Ash Water Oil:
Why the Church needs a new form of monasticism

Ned Lunn

The Society of the Holy Trinity
2020

Copyright © 2020 by Society of the Holy Trinity

All rights reserved. This book or any portion thereof may not be reproduced or used in any manner whatsoever without the express written permission of the publisher except for the use of brief quotations in a book review or scholarly journal.

First Printing: 2020

ISBN 978-0-244-86592-4

Society of the Holy Trinity,
London.

Dedication

In memory of
Sarah Lunn
1986-2018

To Tim & Clare Watson and Dave & Jo Young
who have all heard too much about this book and remained
supportive of me and the material.

Contents

Acknowledgements

This book has taken a long time to compile and create. It has taken many forms over the years and evolved slowly. This means that there has been so many people who have journeyed alongside me as I have been writing it. Too many, in fact, to name them all. Too many people have patiently listened to me explore the themes of this book and tightened my understanding of the subject matter. Too many people have inspired me to go deeper into the topics and challenged me to rethink things that seemed simple to me.

There are, of course, some specific people who have remained constant throughout and it is those people that I'd like to mention and offer my humblest appreciation of.

Ian Mobsby and the wider New Monastic movement has been, as I state in the book, a community of communities to me over the years. Ian, particularly has encouraged me to grow in understanding and experience of the emerging religious communities. It was him that first introduced me to this over a decade ago and it has been him who has invited me to gatherings and seen in me something that I struggled to see for myself. I now have the privilege of working alongside Ian as we seek to develop the Society of the Holy Trinity, an Anglican collaboration of new monastic communities. I am grateful to him for challenging me to write this book.

As part of the birthing of the Society of the Holy Trinity, I gathered and established a community in York in the hope of growing an expression of the religious life. Although it didn't have time to fully take root, the conversations I had with those beautiful people have shaped this book and, indeed, the Society itself. Our fragile community, for the short time we were together helped me immeasurably understand what it was God was leading me to write. Many people have contributed to the actual writing of this book: David Shervington, from SCM, for offering advice on structuring and editing, Eve Ridgeway, for your intelligent, passionate friendship and encouragement to pursue publication of this book and the many others who have said they wanted to read this book… now you have it!

It is the many communities that I have been a part of that have continued to shape me and my understanding of God's Church and why it needs new forms of monasticism to lead it through the challenges of cultural change at this time. Here I am thinking of Cranmer Hall, Durham, where I first experienced intentionality in community and discipleship, and the community of families at Brass Thill. I am also thinking of Acomb Parish Church, York, where I served my curacy and first began to explore the possibility of New Monasticism taking root within the parish context. I am, however, thinking most particularly of my current community, Saint Peter's, Greenhill.

Early on in my time I used the structure and material from this book as a sermon series through Lent and Easter. They patiently received my passionate plea for the universal Church and many of them joined me to preach on the topics. I have been inspired with the way in which they engaged in this material and it has explicitly changed because of them. I want to particularly thank, the Popplewells, the Hayes and the Rowlands who have been particularly significant to me as I sought to live out this radical call to community. Particular thanks to Michelle for proofreading and for Bess for pre-reading it.

Another community, although it gathers for an intense few days each year, is my peer support group from Cranmer Hall, inappropriately named 'Morning Glory'. These four men have watched me grow and change over the years since we first met each Wednesday morning. They have often been the ones who have sharpened my ministry and honed my vocation with me. Matt, Kuhan and Russell are men of great integrity and I love them very much. Andy Stinson stands out as the one who has committed to me and my thinking. It is him and Cat, his wife, who have spoken particularly into this book from this wonderful community of brothers.

To my family who have shaped my understanding of the concept of 'family'; thank you. It is my Mum, however, who has been a constant inspiration and encouragement. I thank her for all those qualities that make me, me. She gave to me a commitment to integrity and honesty. She has encouraged the prophetic voice within me; to speak out against falsehoods or confusion. She taught me to be a teacher and instilled within me a passion for learning, growing and transformation. She continues to give me hope in our Heavenly Father we both love and serve with our whole lives.

God blessed me also with an adopted family when I married Sarah. The Birkinshaws continue to be my safest home and safest rest. These last years have been the toughest for all of us as we cared for Sarah in her final months and saying goodbye to her in 2018. They have been the best people to journey the road of grief with, even when we have had to journey some parts alone. They gave to me the greatest gift of my life and continue to help me to be thankful for her every day. Words cannot express my gratitude and love to you, Mummy, Daddy, Pete and Isobel.

Of all my friends, along with Andy Stinson, there have been two particular families that have been the most like family to me and it is to them that I dedicate this book: the Watsons and the Youngs. Tim and Clare, Dave and Jo, you have informed this book in so many ways I cannot begin to point them all out. In conversation, in experiences, in the commitment that you have shown to me and to Sarah when she was alive. You share this passion for the Church and how new forms of community can lead the way into her health. With Andy and Cat, you remain the greatest friends anyone could be blessed to have. You have seen me in the many different states of change and have remained faithful to me. You drew closer when many moved away. You held me in my darkest of times and have shown what it is to be community. I have wept more tears with you, laughed harder with you, enjoyed your hospitality and have invested more of myself in friendship with you than anyone else. Your children are my children and to them, Evie, Lucie, Toby, Anna, Isaac and Nathan, I offer my life to serve them in love that they may grow to full maturity in Christ.

Finally, Sarah. Sarah made me the man I am. It was her who gifted me with the people in my life. She was the lightness and joy to my heaviness and depth. She reminded me of Jesus, every moment of our life together and I will never be able to express, not with all the words and understanding in the world, how much I loved her, was grateful for her and how much I miss her. This book would not be without her dedication, commitment and love for me. Her encouragement had more impact upon me than anyone else. I only wish that she could have been here to see this book finally published and to hear her speak glowingly of it despite her never going to read it… she'd have waited for the audiobook.

Foreword

An Ancient Future Vision
for new forms of Christian community

Thirty-three years ago, I as a young radical atheist was dragged by some friends from Sixth Form College to go and visit the Taizé Community in Burgundy, France. I did not know consciously then, but I was spiritually hungry, and there was something about the mix of a refreshed form of monastic spirituality, Christian community, the rhythm of work, study, meals, dialogue and participative and mystical forms of prayer and worship that catapulted me to the beginning of a lifelong spiritual longing and search. Soon after this experience and in connection with a number of early Church of England missional experiments (which became Fresh Expressions of Church), opened up a form of Christianity and a path that was relevant and authentic for unchurched spiritual seekers like me. This refreshed form of monastic and mendicant spirituality became known as New Monasticism or the New Monastic movement starting out in the United States and soon named what had been happening across the UK and Europe from the aftermath of the Second World War.

As part of this journey I have now been involved in a number of missional forms of Christian community that have included two new monastic communities that I helped to found. In this journey I became good friends with Ned Lunn the author of this important book in the ever-growing library concerning New Monasticism who has been a soul friend and fellow vision keeper. I have been enriched by Ned's interest particularly in the Benedictine Monastic Rule drawing on his background and fusion of Roman Catholicism and the Charismatic renewal.

This book I think really grapples with the theology and practical implications of the near impossible task of seeking to form a deep and living approach to a refreshed engagement with Monastic spirituality. Ned seeks to do this whilst holding back from the dangers of 'dumbed down' or 'monastic-light' spirituality that can end up being overly romantic and consumeristic rather than the challenge of living a rhythm of life involving worship, work, study, loving action and rest. We remember that Benedict wrote his rule to try and help new Christians face a deeper form of discipleship drawing on a monastic model that led to major reforms of ecclesial community and identity across the western world of the time.

We remember also that it was monastic forms of Christian community that helped the Church re-contextualise from premodernity into modernity. I think it is no coincidence that it is resurgent forms of church inspired by monastic spirituality that seek to resource a thoroughly weakened church from modernity into post-modernity and post-secularisation.

The three movements of this book, 'Ash, Water and Oil' I think reflect metaphorically an interpretation of some of the DNA of a monastic spiritual inheritance as received in a particularly Anglican interpretative context. We remember that there is a monastic spirituality at the heart of this ecclesial form, the book of Common Prayer after all was compiled from adaptations of a monastic daily office where the vision of the reformers of the 16th and 17th centuries were to make parish churches monasteries of ordinary people gathered in particular localities.

The other key aspect of this book also draws on a deep Trinitarianism and the insights of the more Eastern Christian Church around the monastic ecclesial community as a living dynamic body shaped and led by the Holy Spirit which like Ned I do believe lies at the heart of the religious life as shaped in both the Western and Eastern contexts. I believe this is why monasticism has always punched above its weight throughout history and why it has always been a renewing and reforming movement from its inception in the founding desert communities, Mothers and Fathers of Alexandria and Syria.

I hope you enjoy this book as much as I have, and I hope its essence and breadth inspires you to reimagine how forms of re-imagined monastic spirituality can resource and deepen the challenge of what it means to follow the way of Christ in all chaos and uncertainty of the 21st Century.

Ian Mobsby
February 2020.

Preface

This book has taken on many forms over the years of writing. As I prepare to finally release it into the hands of strangers to stand on its own, I am caused to reflect on those many evolving shapes and ask, 'what remains the unchangeable DNA of this work?' It started out as a dissertation on ensemble theatre and models of Christian communities, a blog about how the Rule of St Benedict might renew the shape of parochial ministry and a handful of written critiques of articles from and about Fresh Expressions and New Monasticism. I can see, now I am reading it, that there remains an unswerving desire to express a vision for the unifying of the Church and receiving the gift of the Church from God to His people.

The Church has taken quite a battering over my lifetime, and I'm sure prior to it as well. It is regularly criticized for being slow, unwieldly, unnecessarily dogmatic, restrictive, stuffy, irrelevant, etc. The curses spoken over the Bride of Christ have been so constant that it is rare to hear her speak positively of herself. She has become so self-critical that she has begun to talk only of a complete make-over akin to surgical enhancements and distortions.

This book is my first attempt to retell the Church's story so that she might recapture her beauty seen through the eyes of her Beloved, Christ. I believe the ones who have historically reminded the Body of Christ of her beloved-ness and beauty have been the monastics who have, like Christ, committed their whole lives to seeking her flourishment and praying for her health. Our problem is that they have done so secretly and privately for too long and I hope, in some small way, the New Monastic Movement, and indeed this book, may be an invitation for them to speak publicly over the Church, afresh, "You are the beautiful Bride, whom Christ loves and gave Himself for."

Over the years of writing, I have discovered a particularity of my style which I have learnt to embrace but that does requires pointing out to potential readers. I am, it turns out, a hybrid between academic and poet. Not only do I love going to great lengths to explore complex issues (even if I don't do it very well), I also love the forms and patterns of language sound and are experienced. I tell you this merely to suggest, as you read this work, that the form and choice of words are just as much part of the writing as the content. You can enjoy one if you don't enjoy the other but, of course, I'd rather you enjoyed both! It does also mean that words and phrases are repeated at different points deliberately and intentionally. This use of motifs is integral to holding the work together and giving it a dynamic that I hope also communicates the dynamic of my Trinitarian God.

Ned Lunn
Ash Wednesday 2020

Introduction

It started with me…

My friend Tim and I share a love of Ash Wednesday; the day that begins the Lenten journey towards Holy Week. I'm not sure what makes this day so special for me, whether it is some deep echo from my Roman Catholic upbringing and the sensory stimulating, sacramental service each year or whether the day plays to my naturally more earthy and raw view of the world, I cannot tell. What I do know is that the imagery sings for me, it touches me deep within my being.

Some years ago, whilst I was training for ordained ministry, a group of us gathered to mark Ash Wednesday and I was asked to bring a reflection. I felt called on that occasion to outline the fundamentals of the day and its important place within the rhythm of the liturgical year. It was whilst I prepared for that reflection that my eyes were opened to a much broader narrative; a narrative that sweeps over the forty days of Lent to Palm Sunday, the seven days of Holy Week and then fifty days from Easter Sunday to Pentecost. In this liturgical narrative I saw the story of the dust of our being transforming into living beings. I saw Pentecost in a new light as I reflected on the phoenix-like transformation as the disciples are raised from the ashes and the flame of life relit.

"We are dust caught in the wind of the Spirit." I preached, "We dance because God blows on the ashes of our life with His power. We must remember we are dust, but dust that can, by God's grace, do amazing things."

Over the years, as I have returned to this poetic theme, I have felt called to delve deeper into it and dig out more of its importance. One year my wife and I found ourselves on holiday with my friend Tim and his wife for Ash Wednesday. Knowing that

Tim and I both loved the beauty of the day we decided to celebrate it together. I got to work thinking about how we might creatively mark the occasion and started with this idea of bookending the evening with the ash cross and, at the end, an oil cross for commissioning. It was at that moment it hit me: on Ash Wednesday we mark ourselves with a cross of ash, at Pentecost we are commissioned to service, the symbol used for that is an oil cross on the forehead but in the middle of these two rituals stands Easter, a time traditionally set aside to baptize new believers and we share in that by marking ourselves with a cross of water.

From these three crosses I began to see a Trinitarian shape to the liturgical journey. The imagery of each point of that trajectory from Ash Wednesday to Pentecost gave a depth to the others that made my awareness and understanding of God richer. What does it mean to believe in a God revealed to us in His creative, redeeming and sanctifying actions in the world? I began to see myself placed in a different story than that presented to me by the world; one that led me away from the ashes of death instead of towards the dust from which we came.

This poetic narrative began to shape the rest of my life of faith and my theology began to hang off the resonances of these liturgical occasions. This book is the fruit of my reflections on the annual pilgrimage from Ash Wednesday to Pentecost that draws us to see God's revelation of Himself to humanity as Creator, Redeemer and Sanctifier of the Church. Each section is named after the three crosses of ash, water and oil and encompass the theological insights I believe they hold and each section begins with a parable to draw us into this new story God invites us to inhabit.

This book is also about an emerging movement in the Church which I have been blessed to be caught up in called, 'New Monasticism'. What is contained within these pages, I hope, will be a small gift, not only to the many communities exploring this evolving vocation, but to the whole Church as we seek to faithfully follow Christ in a new cultural landscape. New Monasticism has been attempting to articulate to the wider Church what God is doing amongst us for many years. There have been several difficulties with doing this: one issue has been that it always seems too early to name or consolidate shared experiences, maybe out of fear that once it is named it will stagnate or evaporate (I pray that this will not be the case here). The second is that there has been incoherence and inconsistent expressions of this developing movement.

Some of the people I have had the privilege of travelling with on this journey have made life-long commitments/vows to the religious life in different traditions but are seeking renewal in vocations to the devoted life. Others are parish ministers, ordained and lay, who long for a deeper and richer experience of community and discipleship within that service. Still others are pioneers with a specific call to establish new expressions of church and have found themselves exploring what has come to be known as 'New Monasticism'.

It started, for me, in Durham as I trained for ordained ministry. I had arrived in a city steeped in the ancient tradition of the Church, with the history of the Celtic, monastic saints literally carved into the landscape. Ever since I was small I have been sensitive to place, atmospheres and environments. I grew up in a theatrical family who were actively involved in creating performances and it meant that I was exposed, from a young age, to nuanced experiments of performative experiences. As a practitioner myself, later on in my life, I developed a style that aimed to achieve some universal, 'total' theatre experience. Many of my productions took classic texts out of their historical contexts and, instead of doing what contemporary companies often do and placed them into a different historical or geographical context, I created a deliberate a-contextual setting. I wanted to draw a community of strangers together into a new space and time which none of them could 'own' in order to find commonality in the new space. I would do this by intentionally shaping the atmosphere and environment in which the story is told. Later I would have my aim expressed by the Roman Catholic priest and missionary to Tanzania, Vincent Donovan, as he described his view of evangelism.

> … the unpredictable process of evangelization, [is] a process leading to the new place where none of us has ever been before. When the gospel reaches a people where they are, their response to that gospel is the church in a new place, and the song they will sing is that new, unsung song, that unwritten melody that haunts all of us.[1]

The story remains the same, the characters and the text, unchanged. The placing of the experience, its atmospheric background, the environment in which it is told, shifts the focus and a new song is found. It was in the new environment, the atmospheric background of the historic and, in this case, monastic saints that the gospel became new for me. The monastic lens that I now saw the gospel, discipleship and mission through became, for my faith, the all-encompassing vision.

It started, for me, when I was growing up in the modern Roman Catholic tradition, in a church that was influenced, during my time, by the worship style of the Taize community. It was this deeply experiential, contemplative, theatrical, mystery-laden encounter with the Divine that marked me from an early age. So, in Durham, relinquishing my professional life in the theatre that I had left to take up my vocation, I became fascinated with expressions of worship that were atmospheric and experiential. New Monasticism, expressed first by the Northumbria Community and its Celtic inspiration and later by Ian Mobsby in his urban, arts based form, drew out from me the historic, universal, tradition; marrying the old and the new/fresh. It is this 'marrying', this

[1] Vincent Donovan, *Christianity Rediscovered* (London: SCM Press, 2009) p.xix

seeking for a universal, 'total' experience that I return to again and again. It is the idea that there might be a theory for everything, an a-contextual way of experiencing the gospel of Jesus that will unite us all to know the depth of the truth of God that inspires me in the work you hold in your hand.

In the search for a-contextual productions of classic texts I discovered that one must remain faithful to the words chosen by the writer. If the context demands a change in the text then it is not a-contextual. This consideration of words has also seeped into my ministry, particularly in the engagement with liturgy. There is a trend in the Church to make liturgy contextually relevant and specific. Although I see the great merit of this, there is also much to be said of changing how liturgy is performed and not just changing the liturgy itself. This is particularly important when it comes to the Eucharistic liturgy, which unites us with the universal Church; historic and geographic. Unity is lost and catholicity is diminished when we shape our liturgy around a specific context; however pastorally significant it may be to do so at certain times and circumstances.

In choosing the three narrative themes that begin and run through each section I have selected words that have been used, throughout Church history, to describe God's salvific activity in the world. These words may well carry with them particular, challenging cultural baggage for some and it could be argued that I should re-contextualise them for a modern audience, but I hope that you can understand why I have chosen not to. I have opted instead to a-contextualise them as much as possible in the hope to keep us, the Church, united as brothers and sisters in the universal Church.

The New Monastic movement in Britain is a loose collection of groups who have identified a desire for more intentional community than that which is offered through traditional forms of church gathering. There is no stringent entry policy to this 'network'/movement; it is better seen as an association. Even when a group identifies themselves in the category of 'New Monasticism' it doesn't bind them to another group who have also chosen to name themselves as such. In this way the movement remains self-governing and flexible and it works... sort of.

Accountability is covered for most of these groups through independent means but is not enforceable. Communities should seek to have an outsider to oversee or converse with the community to ensure safeguarding of its members and that relationships remain healthy as the group grows and evolves together. These relationships are based on trust and so the selection of a spiritual companion for a community can be a risky one.

The connection between individual groups and communities is a free choice too. A group can, if they choose, be independent and get on with doing what they're doing and being what they're being without interaction with another group. This choice, however, can lead to a sense of isolation and/or blind egotism, not to mention the spending of energy re-inventing of the metaphorical wheel! Most want to learn from others as they become acutely aware of the challenges that face intentional community. At these times they reach out and discover the joy of journeying with others who share something of what they are living through. Again, these relationships between groups/communities are self-selecting and so carry with them potential dangers. The concern I have is that of the blind leading the blind when there are communities that, although still learning and emerging, have journeyed terrain before and so can steer with wisdom and experience. There are, of course, the traditional established and recognized communities of the religious life in Britain who are the best placed to speak into the experiences of these newer communities from their own sense of vocation. Indeed, it is the challenge set by their way of life which gives me greatest pause and deep concern when discussing the New Monastic movement. What is 'new' about what we are doing?

At the heart of this concern around the New Monastic movement is that we who are part of it want to remain connected with the world in some areas of our life but not in others; we want to remain in control and choose the sacrifices and changes we experience. The sacrifice of the community is self-selecting to suit our individual needs and what we think is right for us. Are we falling short of the ultimate hurdle which distinguishes our, ultimately, secular life and that of the traditional religious life? Does New Monasticism encourage people to remain individualistic consumers whilst giving the impression that we're living radically different lifestyles?

I'm more than aware that we all have unique vocations due to what God wants of us in our different contexts, with our personalities and experiences. Some of us are ready and blessed to be called to the religious life practiced over the centuries in the different traditions. Some of us, though, feel called to that way of life but find ourselves in families and relationships which also seem to be God-given. Some of us are called to ordained ministry within a more parochial context and, at the same time, some form of more intentional life. There seems to be several different shapes and models emerging all naming themselves something slightly different in order to distinguish themselves. 'Missional Communities', 'Hubs', 'Home Groups', 'Organic Communities', 'New Monasticism', or any other unique name for a group who have a particular shape and call on its members. Some would say,

"It works… sort of."

Discipleship and mission must be contextual. Where you find yourself must impact how you live out your faith and mission. The Holy Spirit calls us to particular tasks at particular times in particular places but the source of strength and call must remain fixed in the same God. Although the expression of faith has adapted to different cultures and language, the faith remains steadfast. It is the tension between the rootedness of tradition and the fresh expressions of faith and mission which keeps a sense of life. A balanced life is one lived in tension. Again, it is the receipt of the universality of the gospel story that must go into new contexts to birth new churches.

What I want to advocate in these pages is a uniting of all these new and different expressions of discipleship and community. I know there are many who will disagree and see this endeavor as foolish, unnecessary or, at worst, aggressively totalitarian.

"What works for one, might not work for another," some might proclaim but it is the implicit individualism running through that and similar ideas that is at the heart of my concern. There is a difference between shared principles and homogeny. As an ex theatre practitioner, I often use the example of different actors performing the same character; let's say Hamlet, for example. It's the same words, the same narrative, the same character but Laurence Olivier's portrayal is vastly different to that of Adrian Lester's and his distinct from David Tennant's, etc. ad nauseum. The thing that changes is the context: the time, the place, the people (the cast, the creative team and the audience) and what they bring and how they interact with each other. The script, the story, the structure is all identical but the context changes how it is lived on stage.

As much as I desired an a-contextual presentation of a text/narrative, the audience will all bring with them a cultural lens through which they will receive the story. It is not the receipt of the story that I was trying to control but, rather, the telling. I desired an audience, with varying and, sometimes, conflicting worldviews to be brought together around an experience. The aim of the theatre, as it remains of the Church, for me, is leading the scattered and divergent to gather and connect and to lead all to leave changed by that experience. The challenge is how we speak to multiple people at the same time. Is there a way to be one and yet many?

I can see that there may be some who will also argue that 'pinning down' or 'fencing in' these exciting, new discoveries hinders them from being 'organic' and 'adaptable' that keeps a movement streamlined and flexible, able to move to new places and reach wider people. It strikes me though that, as well as an individualistic desire to be 'different' and pioneering, there may also be an underlying addiction to novelty and relevancy. Are we so invested in an 'attractional' mindset that we feel the need to continually change our way of life to appeal to our world? Are we not avoiding the narrow path in order to fit more people down the wider path or renovating our home in order to be more enticing to those who may or may not want to live there? Should we be placing 'relevance' as our highest priority in evangelism and mission over and above, let's say, 'prophetic counter-culturalism'?

> …Jesus calls us to be peculiar but also to engage in the world we find ourselves in. We are to be relevant nonconformists. We are to develop countercultural habits and norms (the Sermon on the Mount) and live them in the midst of an insane world. Much of the church, however, in its search for relevance, falls in love with the world, its methods of communication, and its patterns of consumerism, and sacrifices holy nonconformity for the sake of cultural relevancy.[2]

Oscar Romero wrote in 1965,

> The Church, then, is in an hour of aggiornamento, that is, of crisis in its history. And as in all aggiornamenti, two antagonistic forces emerge: on the one hand, a boundless desire for novelty, which Paul VI described as "arbitrary dreams of artificial renewals"; and on the other hand, an attachment to the changelessness of the forms with which the Church has clothed itself over the centuries and a rejection of the character of modern times. Both extremes sin by exaggeration. Unconditional attachment to what is

[2] Shane Claiborne, *Jesus for President: politics for ordinary radicals* (Michigan: Zondervan, 2008) p. 238-240

> old hampers the Church's progress and restricts its "catholicity"... The boundless spirit of novelty is an impudent exploration of what is uncertain, and at the same time unjustly betrays the rich heritage of past experiences... So as not to fall into either the ridiculous position of uncritical affection for what is old, or the ridiculous position of becoming adventurers pursuing "artificial dreams" about novelties, the best thing is to live today more than ever according to the classic axiom: think with the Church.[3]

My own vocation has revolved around this reconciliation and synthesizing of ideas and traditions of which Romero writes. I have a naturally systematic mind which links concepts together into a framework which enables one to sit alongside another for the mutual flourishing of both. This has meant that when I am placed at the core of my calling, I can find myself torn and divided internally as I attempt to hold onto difference. I am, in that sense, a priest caught within the tensions of life, crying out to God to unite all things in Christ.

Once, when I was struggling particularly with the pain of this ministry, I was prayed for by an older man who had walked the journey of faith longer than I had. He told me of a picture he felt he had received from God for me. It was of a mountain goat up in the craggy and seemingly inhospitable mountains. Looking down into the valley he saw there was lush green grass with sheep and goats happily feeding but the Lord spoke to me through this. The man finished by saying,

"It feels like God built you for the mountain terrain."

I have reflected often on this picture and drawn comfort from it when I have found myself in spiritual wilderness, barrenness, in conflict and rough seas. I get uncomfortable when I do find a

---

[3] Oscar Romero, quoted in Morrozzo Della Rocca, Roberto, *Oscar Romero: prophet of hope* (London: Dalton, Longman and Todd, 2015) p.22-23

settled place, a place of comfort for I have always ministered in places and times of uncertainty and conflict. It does seem like God has built me to thrive in the wild but even the mountain goats need a place of refuge. Psalm 104 reads, 'The high mountains are for the wild goats; the rocks are a refuge for the coneys.' (Psalm 104:18) I survive but in a different way to how the sheep of the green pasture survive down in the valley. I am one who finds himself, more often than not, in isolated viewpoints. I don't fit. This always runs dangerously close to the temptation to be different and contrary and I am on constant watch to not fall into that trap. I know that is part of where God must hold me close and be my refuge and I know that I am not alone in this vocation.

Other 'New Monastics' have a similar sense of tension and others, on both sides of the divide we try to inhabit, are discovering the imperative articulated by Romero back in 1965. I agree that the Spirit blows where it will, and the Church has suffered by its slowness to catch up with God. I agree that definition can exclude some who might have otherwise moved further in if they were encouraged to, or rather if they were not discouraged by boundaries. I agree that most communities who identify with this 'New Monastic' call, whatever that means for them, remain fragile and embryonic. And I totally agree that the reason that Church doesn't work for increasing numbers of people is because of our culture's anxiety, fear and disapproval of institution.

It still comes down, for me, however, to a desperate need for the gospel to challenge individualistic consumer culture and not collude with it. Structures and frameworks are needed for a sense of security and refuge. It is not sustainable to constantly live in uncertainty, risk and vulnerability; we need shelter, even if it is just a tent that is moveable. It is interesting to reflect on the use of tents in the Bible. Tents give people a resting place in a landscape of wilderness. Tents are used as 'home' when you are being called to be nomadic. Tents give you the space to feel safe when the rest of your life is danger and risk. Paul uses this image to describe our earthly bodies on earth and to encourage us to see ourselves as belonging to another place.

As the Church continues to traverse its post-Christendom landscape where the terrain has dramatically changed and new ways of living and, let's be honest, surviving must be sought, those of us called and experienced in dwelling in wilderness could help. It is a vocation which is not new but is found in the ancient monastic tradition: the desert Fathers and Mothers, Augustine as the Roman Empire fell, Benedict during the Dark Ages, Francis, Ignatius, the Wesleys, the Oxford Movement. At this point in our history, like in previous eras, the Church should pay attention to the emerging forms of the monastic charism for its own renewal and reformation.

For me, a Rule of Life has the potential to hold me in the creative tension between the fresh and new and the rooted and traditional. As I have explored different Rules and studied the charisms of different communities what fascinates and excites me is that, despite being different, they share similar central calls; they name them different things but they're essentially the same. I'm talking about principles they live by not the practices they perform.

What I want to propose to my fellow wilderness dwellers is a set of virtues to seek to inhabit as part of our tents. I wonder what would emerge if we acknowledged together, a sense that the New Monastic call is, like our brothers and sisters of the religious life, a commitment to 'stability, conversion and obedience' (RB 58:17).[4] To explicitly seek to live a life rooted somewhere or with someone; no matter what the spiritual weather is like, no matter what temptations afflict you. To respond to the call to stay and remain faithful. Secondly, to continually engage in the work of personal change; to turn away, step by step, from the things of this world to the Kingdom of God; to intentionally become, in different

[4] Some may want to interpret them as the traditional vows of 'chastity, poverty and obedience' but I see them as interchangeable. I explore this in detail in Chapter 8.

circumstances and in different ways, more and more Christ-like, poor and dependent on God. And, thirdly, to desire to place yourself under the decisions of something or someone else; to curb that deeply human temptation to be in control of ourselves and our decisions; to hold onto the power in our own lives.

There has been, in recent years, an increased use of the term 'Rule of Life' within the Church of England as individuals, parishes and even dioceses use it to give focus and vision to their lives. These Rules, however beautifully shaped and well intentioned, fail in one significant and fundamental way: there is no articulation of discipline. Discipline comes from the same root word as 'disciple' and we in the West have shied away from this corrective aspect of discipleship since the social liberalisation of the 1960s. It has been to our detriment. Those committed to a religious order are rightly concerned by the adoption of this language without the important accountability of living under their own order's Rule. The Church and, at times, New Monastics are happy to 'play' at radical discipleship without ever experiencing the necessary death of ego and autonomy. At its very heart, this book is my personal plea that the Church embraces the discipline of a real Rule of Life, to understand the welcoming and necessary constraints of it and to become ready for her Bridegroom. All of our lives should be continually shaped by a daily commitment to the corrective principles of stability, conversion and obedience worked out in lived experience within our communities.

Unlike New Monasticism's forebears within the established religious communities this vocation to the threefold virtues is being placed within family life, secular employment and work and in the parochial expression (or ecumenical equivalents) of Christ's Church.[5] My impression is that the New Monastic movement is, for

---

[5] I appreciate this is not unlike the oblate vocation within the monastic tradition, but the oblates remain distant from the communities they commit to as they live out their vocation. What the New Monastic movement is finding is the need for these oblate-like disciples to be rooted in a contextual community.

now, located between the traditional religious life and that of the rest of the Church in order to enable the mutual flourishing of both. I'm happy to concede it may be a temporary call, but a temporary call that is a Spirit-initiated act being used for the renewal of the whole Church and the reinvigorating of the monastic houses with fresh vocations to the life of devotion.

I will be exploring the three principles of stability, conversion and obedience in turn and asking how we might live these out in the midst of 'ordinary' discipleship and how they can help us shape our life together in a more balanced tension. I want to explore how the interplay between these three values also begins to breakdown the tendency to see the world in binary ways: old or new, margins or mainstream, prayer or action and brings about a more perichoretic life mirroring the life of the Trinitarian God in whom we have our being. Esther de Waal begins her chapter on stability in 'Seeking God' with a helpful description of the relationship between these three monastic vows.

> The beauty of the rule [of St Benedict] is the way in which the three vows... all interrelate. Even if we separate them and look at them one by one we shall discover that common themes and underlying threads bind them together, and that there is an inner logic by which they constantly illuminate, deepen and depend on each other.[6]

Although this triptych of stability, conversion and obedience, is, arguably less linear than the theological story of creation, redemption and sanctification, each principle has been placed, in this book, alongside one of these themes and will be linked. This doesn't mean that one of the other two could not, quite easily, have been paired with any of the other theological themes. I hope that in placing each alongside a particular theme both will become richer in their interactions.

---

[6] Esther de Waal, *Seeking God: the way of St. Benedict* (London: Faith Press, 1985) p.55

I have heard, and even used myself, a domestication of the language of 'Rules of Life'. We present it to people as suggestive waymarkers rather than legal requirements and translate 'Rule' as gentle offers to how we dream of living. The historic Rules of Augustine, Benedict and Francis, however, in their different ways, make explicit demands on the life of those lived under them. There is an expectation within the pages that these will be upheld or there will be discipline; even if that discipline is the public acknowledgement that one has fallen short or strayed from the guidance. The adoption of a Rule of Life, if it is to have a similar effect on adherents' lives, must have clear accountability as to how it will be implemented. Too often those who have committed their lives to a Rule have genuine and understandable questions over those of us who develop new Rules and place little to no discipline in place for when the Rule is not followed. As we explore the three-fold commitments to stability, conversion and obedience we will draw out the benefit and blessing of making choices and commitments and how New Monasticism might grow in this area, in order to teach the wider Church about what means to commit our lives to following Christ on the narrow path.

Finally, there has been one image that is shared amongst these emerging intentional communities, almost universally: Rublev's icon of the Trinity. This image has become somewhat of a cliché amongst the New Monastic movement, but it is important to note it and to name it. This (re)discovery and fresh exploration of Trinitarian theology is clearly key to the movement and it is because of this that I feel the insights that my own reflections have revealed might be useful to us all.

If we are, to heed Romero's words, 'to think with the Church' then we must engage in rigorous theological learning. This is why we will be beginning each section with a chapter on, what I hope is, a reasserting of orthodox belief. As we proceed through the narrative presentation of our faith, I pray we will be drawn deeper and deeper into the mystery of our Triune God. Like an icon I hope that we will find ourselves stepping through a threshold into an experience of the community of God.

As well as Rublev's icon and the shared values/principles of life, there has emerged some shared practices. These practices seem so obvious that it is hardly worth noting but I hope that in naming them here and placing them before New Monastic communities, both established and developing, as waymarks, we may begin to draw closer together. These practices are: prayer/worship, learning/study, mission/service and hospitality.

Wherever I come across new missional/monastic communities I find that they naturally structure their lives around an intentional rhythm of prayer and worship. Yes, of course all Christian communities pray but in these smaller evolving communities, prayer takes on new significance as their dependence on God is more obvious and immediate. Their life of prayer is also characteristically rhythmic with the common use of an 'office', a set structure and wording that all may say together whether they are meeting in the same place or not. The re-discovery of liturgical prayer acts as an introduction as well as a binding agent within these communities. What I mean by that is when people join a community, they can learn how to pray with the community quickly and in a highly explicit way; there is no awkwardness as newcomers ask "What do I say? What is acceptable here? What language do I use?" These prayers also enable and equip anyone in the community to lead the prayers almost immediately and breaks down any implicit dependency. The daily office also binds a community together with the understanding that the prayers you are speaking to God are being spoken by the rest of your community with you; you are not alone.

These new communities are also typically open to ongoing learning. There is within the DNA of this emerging movement a deep appreciation for the unknown and developing patterns of discipleship with an emphasis on what St. Paul calls 'the renewing of our minds.' Learning, study, reflection, dialogue, these are hallmarks of the new missional/monastic communities. Where many other forms of Christian community fall down is an implicit assumption that 'we've made it.' There is, within the New Monastic movement, an overt emphasis on questions shaping the life of any community. A Rowan Williams quote may well chime with many who find themselves within a new missional/monastic community,

> Jesus answers our questions, but he also questions our answers.[7]

At the centre of this learning is a renewed commitment to vulnerability both intellectual and emotional. This is expressed through a deep engagement with dialogue/conversation often over a meal. Before I talk about this dedication to the task of hospitality, I'd like to add a brief comment about the place of reconciliation within these communities. Although few communities name reconciliation as an intentional aspect of their life together many of them are places of deep forgiveness and healing and it is, I would argue, because they are passionate about real, deep and vulnerable sharing; being open to transformation of their ideas and worldview as well as the activity of their lives.

These new communities have been birthed from the need to recapture the missional heart of God within His Church and so there is an imperative to serve and proclaim the good news of Jesus in the places they find themselves in. These communities have a deep awareness of their sent-ness with a focus on asking how, as disciples, they can be salt and light to their neighbourhoods and networks. Mission, for these communities, is a broad term encapsulating the Anglican five marks:

---

[7]I discovered this quote within the Northumbria Community … but cannot find the original reference of where or when Rowan Williams used it.

to proclaim the good news of the kingdom,
to teach, baptize and nurture new believers,
to respond to human need by loving service,
to transform unjust structures of society and
to strive to safeguard the integrity of creation.

Although for some there is a call to proclaim and nurture new believers, for others mission is digging up the soil, preparing the ground for seeds of the gospel to be planted. Mission is both word and deed and requires a balanced, holistic approach to engaging in the culture and lives of those we meet and share life with.

Finally, the shared practice of hospitality, particularly over food, is an important aspect of all these communities and is used both as a place for learning and dialogue as well as a vehicle for mission and outreach. There is a need to explore and articulate why hospitality is a key theme across these communities. I want to offer some reflections as to why, within a deeply Trinitarian understanding of community, hospitality, centred on Rublev's depiction of the visitors at Mamre, must remain a hallmark as we mirror the character of God to one another and to the world.

I will be exploring these practices using a third threefold structure based on the Benedictine formula of prayer, study and service, to suggest that an explicit balance of these practices can encourage a deepening discipleship. Like, the liturgical framework outlined before and the three virtues of stability, obedience and conversion, this practical framework can be seen as a narrative that flows one to another. I want to lean on the wisdom of the fourth century monk, Evagrius of Ponticus, who proposed a three-step course to spiritual formation.

His process of formation consisted of prakitike, theoria physike, and theoria theologike and was written in three books mapping the different disciplines onto the Biblical texts of Proverbs, Ecclesiastes and the Song of Songs. 'Praktike' outlines a form of moral philosophy and essentially means asceticism, a stripping of our own understanding and worldview. 'Theoria physike' is contemplation of the natural world and of the Scriptures and 'theoria theologike' 'is the highest step and indicates the perfect immediate contemplation of the Holy Trinity'[8]. Blossom Stefaniw, in her paper 'Exegetical Curricula in Origen, Didymus, and Evagrius' highlights that 'we cannot know whether and what the order in which these books were taught was.'[9]

There is, I would propose, a strong argument to be made that there is a coherent flow from praktike to theoria theologike via theoria physike. In this formulation we begin with a stilling or silencing of our hearts in prayer enabling us to move into a place of seeing and studying God in the world, through the tangible creation. Having encountered God through nature, other people and Scripture, Evagrius encourages the disciple to allow God to enter their inner life and indwell them.

Like the three virtues above, the practices of prayer, study and service are not confined to being understood purely in this order. I do, however, want to use the theological themes and the virtues to bring out deeper insights of these central practices and Evagrius' journey through the three steps towards discipleship is helpful as a framework. The use of threes throughout this work is not only an aesthetical choice (although I love a good gimmick!) but rather is a celebration of the creative tension created when three dimensions are used instead of just two.

At the heart of our understanding of a Trinitarian God is the belief that God has revealed Himself as a perfect, dynamic balanced entity in which we are shaped and modelled. The Scriptures tell us that we are created in the image of God and Augustine spoke of 'finding his rest' only in God. We were made for three. Three, is indeed, the 'magic number' and has always held

[8] Blossom Stefaniw, "Exegetical Curricula in Origen, Didymus, and Evagrius: pedagogical agenda and the case for neoplatonist influence", Jean Baun, A Cameron, M Edwards and M Vinzent (ed.), Studia Patristica Vol. XIV: papers presented at the fifteenth international conference of patristic studies held in Oxford 2007 (Leuven: Peeters, 2010) p.288

[9] Ibid.

special significance to us. Engineers know that triangles are the strongest shape to build with. Comedians and storytellers understand the natural rhythm of three and in philosophy, Hegel, amongst others, used three in his models of dialectic or discourse; thesis, antithesis and synthesis or, as Hegel, used 'abstract, negative and concrete'. It is this addition of synthesis, a third axis, that brings depth and balance to opposing forces, creating from conflict, beauty and purpose that I want to propose in this book.

My main point through all of what you are about to read is that I have found an a-contextual gospel which structures my life and the life of the Church. I understand more richly my Trinitarian God who is not in conflict with Himself and in whom a peace which passes all understanding exists and the purest love which is exchanged in freedom flows out from and blesses us with His grace. It is possible to be both one and many simultaneously. At the same time, my discipleship is more holistic when I am attentive to my thoughts and personal concept of God, to my behaviours and actions and, simultaneously, to the need of right relationship with others for my emotional wellbeing. It is in the synthesizing of orthodoxy (right thinking/understanding), orthopathy (right feeling/desires) and orthopraxis (right doing/action) that I am fully able to fulfill the great commandment to 'love the Lord your God with all your heart, and with all your soul and with all your might.'[10] (Deut 6:5)

And so, like Donovan, I continue to seek out this new space,

> What we have to be involved in is not the revival of the church or the reform of the church. It has to be nothing less than what Paul and the Fathers of the Council of

[10] In the original Hebrew the 'heart' is labab which is more connected to the mind and will than to emotions as we use it. 'Soul' is a translation of the word naphash which means person or life and is about desires and emotions and 'might' is a translation of od which communicates a physical, bodily force; strength.

> Jerusalem were involved in for their time – the refounding of the Catholic church for our age.[11]

For our time, what does the Catholic, the universal Church, the universal faith look like in our different contexts? I hope these pages may help to tell our shared story again, with an a-contextual background, to draw us together to see, afresh, the power of the gospel for all of creation.

[11] Donovan, *Christianity Rediscovered*, p.xix

ASH

Creation

The Kingdom of God is like a father
who, out of love for his child,
plays a game of 'hide and seek'...

The simple premise of 'hide and seek': one person or group hides and, after a suitable period of time, the other person or group tries to discover where they are hiding. From my experience, children, when learning to play this game, go through the same stages of enlightenment. The child begins by approaching her father excitedly and begs to play.

"Papa. Papa. I've got an idea... let's play hide and seek."

"Ok." He says, "Who's going to count first?"

"You count to ten and I'll go and hide... in my bed."

It is clear that they are no longer playing the classic game of 'hide and seek' but a new version: 'hide and collect'. What is it that makes children think that what they are imagining is going to yield any sort of enjoyment? The father, with a more sophisticated understanding of the game, can see that this is going to quickly become a dull and tedious exercise of counting to ten and going to meet the other player in the designated place of 'hiding'.

Off the child runs to the elected hiding place and the father begins to count.

"One. Two. Three..." As he counts he can hear their child giggling and settling. "Four. Five. Six..." Silence descends on the house except the momentary shuffling of bed sheets upstairs. "Seven. Eight. Nine..." The father slowly begins the ascent, knowing that they need no more time. "Ten. Coming, ready or not."

Does the father go straight to the bed where he knows they are hiding, or does he try and teach them how the 'seeking' part works in this game? He decides to extend the time their child hides to build the anticipation of being found.

"Where could they be? Are they in the bathroom?" Before the father has a chance to open a bathroom door the child jumps from their hiding place with the panache of a magician finishing off a reappearing trick.

"Here I am! Now it's your turn to hide. I'll count to ten... and you can hide behind the sofa."

What part of this game do they understand? They don't understand what hiding is or what it means to seek. The game is no longer 'hide and seek' nor is it 'hide and collect' but rather 'going and meeting' or some such game; the principle of which is to tell people where you are going to meet them and after ten seconds to meet them there.

The child begins counting and now it is the father who must head off to the sofa downstairs. As he approaches the hiding place he considers the role he is playing in this game. He can't start to teach them how to seek if they don't understand what it means to hide. The child may understand the convention of looking in other places before discovering the other person and so the father decides to be a good hider and waits in his hiding place patiently until they find me.

"Ten. Coming, ready or not." The little footsteps trickle down the stairs. "Where are you?" The footsteps get closer. It is clear they are coming straight to the sofa and sure enough, "There you are! I've found you."

"Well done. How did you know where to find me?" The sarcasm lost on the tiny competitor.

"My turn. You count to ten and I'll hide..."

"Don't tell me where you're going to hide. Just go and I'll try and find you without any help. How does that sound?" The look of confusion and as much pity as this small child can muster streaks across their face as if to say, "If you want to but why make it hard for yourself?" So off they totter upstairs, no doubt to the wardrobe in their father's room, the only other hiding place they can think of.

As the father counts it would be understandable to consider stopping this game and returning to something more interesting and adult like, having a conversation or managing the household but, out of love, decides that, however tedious and dull this current 'game' is, his child is enjoying herself and that's all that matters.

The father patiently plods up the stairs and goes through the motions and the script of this inevitable process.

"Where could she be? Is she under this book?"

"Here I am! Ok. Now I'll count and you can hide..." The child begins to struggle to think of a new place to hide now that they've used all the places they know of as 'hiding places'. They decide to go back to the first hiding place. "You can hide in the bed."

"Which bed?"

"My bed, silly." So the counting begins again. Then the father stumbles upon an idea. What if he doesn't hide in the bed but in a new hiding place that his child does not know about? How would they react then? So he deviates from his path to the bed and slips surreptitiously behind the curtain in the child's bedroom.

"Coming, ready or not... Where could he be?" As the child enters the room and heads towards the bed the father can see them through the curtains. They pull the covers from the bed and proudly proclaims, "They you are! Oh... Where are you? Papa?" The sound of slight panic enters their voice. They look around the room and their face is the picture of disappointment and concern. "Mama? Where's Papa?" They run off to get help from another member of the family. The father waits patiently behind the curtain listening to the conversation now going on downstairs.

"Mama, Papa is not in the bed and I told him to hide there while I counted to ten."

"Maybe he's hiding somewhere else." Mama suggests, "Have you looked somewhere else?"

"But I told him to hide in the bed."

"Where else could he be?"

"I got an idea... maybe he's hiding behind the sofa?"

"Why don't you look?"

Behind the curtain the father is enjoying the game that had become predictable and boring as his child now genuinely seeks him. Every time they look in another place the excitement builds. Their seeking becomes more intense and passionate with each failed attempt at finding their beloved Papa. Soon they are upstairs pulling back covers on all the beds, flinging open wardrobes and cupboards, crouching down, stretching up; the search is on!

The energy, however, begins to waiver and the child pauses.

The father sees, from his hiding place, a sullen face begin to appear. His child, whom he loves, is about to start a sulk which, if past experience is anything to go on, will transform quickly into a tantrum and his relationship with them will be over. The remedy is clear; call their name. This acts as a reminder that he will not abandon his child completely, that the game is not over and what they are experiencing is part of the thrill.

"My child" he whispers.

The face lights up and the search continues, this time with more focus and determination. With renewed vigour they fling wide the curtains and with an excitement and pride unmatched by the previous 'finds' they shout through the laughter,

"There you are! I thought I'd lost you! I really had to look that time! I looked under the sofa and in the wardrobe..." They are jumping around and reliving the search, dragging their father around showing him where they had looked and, as if in the same thought, they turn. They look their father in the eyes and says, "I'm so glad I found you. Now it's my turn to hide... I'll be in the wardrobe."

The relationship between God and His people can be seen as a game of 'hide and seek'. Through the Bible this image of hiding and seeking continues to appear; God seeking His people, God's people seeking their Lord, exclamations of fear as God 'hides Himself' and, through it all, God finding the lost and the hidden.

The image of God as Father is so central to Christian theology that it can sometimes feel clichéd by its assertion. We in Western society, so used to this image of the Divine as a loving Father, can forget about its mind-blowing significance. God, Creator, Power beyond all power, source of all being and life is not some distant entity who commands sycophantic underlings to appease His every whim and changeable demands but rather invites His beloved creatures into relationship, as close as two completely distinct beings can.

It was this Father that made us, tenderly crafted us from the materials He had called into existence. Whether we use poetic or scientific language it matters not; from nothing (*ex nihilo*), something appears. For now, I will fall back on my poetic heart and speak in those terms but be assured that the poetry I use expresses a scientific theory for how the unknown beginning, the genesis, occurred.

After a period of time (something also created at that moment of ultimate creation!), one could, if they were there with the ability to understand such concepts, say that the universe had been created. There was life in a plethora of forms and the internal workings of the cosmos had settled, as much as they will do for millennia, into the patterns we now know; day follows night, spring follows winter, the planets rotate around large stars which burn bright and gravity holds things in a constant motion and balance.

On a single planetary body there exists, randomly so it seems, the perfect combinations of states for a more complex life form to be birthed. This is where I may begin to part from some others' understandings of the beginning. I hold to an understanding that in a universe where all seems so balanced and held in perfect tension, randomness seems more than unlikely. Forgive me any ignorance or naivety but I prefer to see beautiful order rather than accident and meaninglessness.

The Father saw what He had brought into existence in all its multiplicity and complexity and anthropomorphically smiled with a pleasure that still resonates and echoes through space, which we feel when we see the miraculous elegance of the stars, the systems and the dance of the planets. Yet He was not satisfied with his work of art. It missed the final flourish that would seal it as incomparable in its perfection: creatures who had the ability to share in His enjoyment.

He chose one of the millions of planets, on the edge of everything, where He would house them. From this vantage point they would grow and be able to view the rest of the work and grasp the sheer magnitude of the project that the Father had lovingly created. On the edge, they would not be distracted by their own importance but would be awestruck with the privilege of the abounding gift of consciousness and closeness with the Divine.

Yes, He could have just called them into existence like the rest of the created order but there was something in creating these creatures by the means by which they will participate in the act of creativity from now on. He began this work with the intention that it would self-grow and develop: this creature would be able to learn and discover. With great love and grace the Father stooped down into the messy dust of the chosen home and began the timely work of shaping such creatures.

He created them and placed within them the potential to reflect His character back to Himself. He wired them to be able to understand Him and to relate to Him; to love like Him. He named them Adam, meaning ruddy/red, and Eve, meaning life-giver. Both were dearly loved by the Father and both together would reflect him through the dust of their existence. Their life was always to be fragile and precarious, deliberately so, in order that they would know where they came from and where they could, without their eternal Father, return to. As a final act of love the Father gave to them freedom and free-will. These gifts meant that the reciprocated connection between creature and Creator would never be forced or obligatorily required.

Early on in the poetic, biblical narrative, Adam and Eve, the apple of God's eye (excuse the pun), the pinnacle of His creation, were placed in the centre of the young, beautiful place they called home; a garden called Eden. Alongside them there was a tree that bore fruit that would bestow upon the eater all knowledge and insight. The power inherent with humanity would be wedded to the capability to dream of all consequences of every action, good and bad.

Why did the Divine make such a foolish and obvious bug in His otherwise perfect system? Freedom is not freedom if there is no choice.

The Father speaks to His children and sets in motion the process of exchanging freely given love; the ultimate experience of life within creation.

"I have given you freedom to do as you choose. I have given to you freedom to explore and discover all I have made; it's all for you. I am with you always and can guide you and instruct you. If you trust me, you will enjoy all the splendours of my creation. In order to exist and flourish in this experiential environment there is one ingredient you will need: you must want to be with me. If you want to be on your own, without me, then all you must do is take the fruit from the tree of Knowledge of Good and Evil. This will mean you can discover your own way around this vast cosmos. What shall it be?"

Within the reality of freedom lies the existence of temptation because temptation is choice. Adam and Eve, when faced with a choice, found themselves tempted to take the fruit. Because of our free will humanity is wired for curiosity, we are made to discover for in discovery is wonder. Our ancestors, when faced with the choice, freely chose the opportunity to become like God. This remains the ultimate choice given to each one of these beloved creatures, made by God; to know ourselves as created or to think of ourselves as gods of our own destiny.

The temptation proved too much for Adam and Eve and they took the fruit and ate it and, in so doing, broke the trusting relationship between them and God. This action was a sign of the conscious decision to trust in their own subjective opinion rather than believe in God's understanding of the world and knowledge of how it works. They decided to be separated and independent from God, to state for themselves,

"His perspective doesn't impact ours. We are enough. My 'self' comes from me and not Him." From that moment on we learnt that we could be whatever we can imagine. Our identity is no longer fixed or rooted. We can cut loose from every shackle and tell any story we want to inhabit. We can play any role; perform any part in the story we create within our own little heads. We put on the mask and limit what others see… who are we kidding? We can limit even what we see of ourselves.

It says, in the story of Adam and Eve, that due to shame, they covered themselves (Gen 3:7). Shame is a deeply felt response when we see ourselves compared to our own potential. Adam and Eve suddenly saw themselves as the dust that they were made of and grasped, for the first time, how limited they were without God. They knew nothing, understood nothing, the whole created reality was overwhelming, and they felt so insignificant. They were not God.

The experience of shame is one of great vulnerability. As the internal story we build around us to feel safe crumbles in the face of overwhelming reality and we feel exposed; naked. In the poetic story, Adam and Eve feel 'naked' and so 'they hid themselves among the trees' (Gen 3:8b); they covered themselves with leaves to feel safe again, but leaves did nothing to sate that insidious sensation of shame as it mutated into guilt, disappointment, sadness and anger.

Then they heard God walking in the garden where they were.

"Coming, ready or not." and the first game of 'hide and seek' begins. God calls out,

"Where are you?"

If God is all knowing and omnipresent why did He ask this question? Were Adam and Eve good hiders? No. Like every child they are acting predictably, and God knows what happened and where they were 'hiding'.

The call of God, for me, is the same as in the game of 'hide and seek' with a child; a coaxing call, a declaration that the person who has made the decision to be hidden and alone is loved by the other person so much that they will come looking in order that a joyful reunion can happen.

The separation in 'hide and seek' acts as a reminder of the joy of being together. The "Where are you?" of God is a statement of intent, "I want to be united and linked with you again. I am rejecting your desire to destroy our intimacy and I am still seeking to be in that form of relationship." For Adam and Eve, who performed a potent sign of division from God, this divine rhetorical question was a provocative call to reconciliation, but their shame had already become pride and they continued to believe that they could fix this. They had forgotten the story and were re-writing it as they go. They had forgotten that they were nothing but dust, raised up by the choice of their Creator and given life.

God knows us. He knows us completely, 'he knows how we were made; he remembers that we are dust.' (Ps 103:14) Why do we still try and hide and imagine that we have the power and intelligence to re-write our stories? We are foolish in this belief. God allows us to 'hide' because He knows it is our desire to be hidden from Him. He allows us to remain hidden, or at least for us to exist in our belief that we are hidden, but we are never hidden from Him. The Psalmist writes, 'Where can I flee [hide] from your presence...' (Psalm 139:7)

Like a loving parent with a child in 'hide and seek' He continues the facade of seeking, knowing where you are. He will go through the motions and the script of the game so that you will experience the power of choosing to hide, to be in control but this is make-believe; fantasy.

Adam and Eve are not the only children to hide from their loving Father in the Bible. Many run from Him and try to hide in shame; Cain, Jacob, David, Jonah, the list goes on. Each time it is shame, in one form or another, that drives them. It is when we don't want to be 'known' through the unfaltering eyes of intimacy that we hide and cover ourselves. We put on the masks and when the masks become shameful, we cover them up and the layers get built up until we're not only hiding from God but, out of fear, we find ourselves hiding from one another and even ourselves.

In our society today we have lost the deep experience of intimate relationships. We have a sexual crisis due to our lack of healthy, balanced, trusting relationships. Violence is the outworking of a deep feeling of losing control; and it's scary! Communities struggle to exist in peace because peace comes when we let go of power and are free to allow others to possess us; to know us. But we don't know who we are because we've been hiding since we first felt the sting of shame. We've been covering ourselves, masking ourselves for so long we have forgotten the freedom of being found by a beloved other.

Yes, we've been hiding, but what makes the masks more difficult to remove is the lies we hear and tell ourselves; that the masks *are* us. We hear or feel that the masks become us and in a way they do. Our personalities are constructed by decisions to accept certain characters or behaviours. The complications of identity evolve quickly and unconsciously from the moment we are conceived. Biology, environment, relationships, experiences, training; it's the way we function and settle within groups. Personality and identity changes depending on who we are around and how we instinctively need to survive in those contexts.

The most pernicious of lies, however, comes when we start to believe that before we were born that we were destined to be a certain thing.

"This is who I am."

There's this underlying belief that we are programmed from conception (or birth, depending on your belief); a default factory setting. Our task is to strip back to the original 'me'.

"This is how I was made."

But what if we remind ourselves that our identity began where Adam and Eve's began; in the dust. We were nothing but fragments and atoms, carbon, minute broken shards of creation. We were made out of love, for love. The problem is that by the time we need to 'find ourselves' we have already forgotten what it feels like to be gazed on by our Creator. It feels as though it should be easy to step out from our hiding place and be found by God but we quickly forget, or rather, we quickly replace the story with one where we remain at the centre.

We are not, despite the depth in which we feel it, the main part in our story! There is one that is better, stronger, more powerful than we will ever be; we forget Him at our peril. Without Him above us we become drunk on our own achievements as a species. We begin to tell ourselves that we can do anything, be anything, form the world into our own dreams and fantasies; we are the main protagonists and we will drive the story. To remind ourselves of our creation, of our createdness, is to place ourselves into the right role in the true story and the story begins with some earth.

Humility is rooted in the Latin *humus*, meaning "ground". I find it helpful to rename it 'grounded'. To be humble is not to become a self-loathing doormat but to possess the true and frank acknowledgement of our standing in the world. When we see humility centred on who we are, what we have done (or not done), how others see us, we remain as self-centred as when we indulge in proud visions of our own importance. Rick Warren puts it as follows,

> Humility is not thinking less of yourself; it is thinking of yourself less.[12]

The first part of the healing required for us and our world is to remember the start of our story. The Father's first response to the breakdown of relationship with His children was inviting them into a process of reconciliation. He did not force negotiations, He lured them with love. When He revealed them and brought them into the light their shame would have increased, and they began to blame one another (how often do we still do this!) The Father gave them an opportunity to be truthful but they both refused, choosing to exist in a different story than reality. The children had decided to stay hidden in their own created world and there is where they would remain.

We still live in that alternative reality. The pattern of their lives has repeated throughout history. This is what the concept of original sin is: we learn from our parents and their generation; we are shaped by them whether we like it or not. They are shaped by the previous generation and so on and so on…

We have chosen to go it alone so many times that the alternative option is almost eradicated from our minds. We no longer engage in the intentionality of choice because we are so used to choosing the same path and the path leads to death; the complete liberation from the source of life itself.

"You are dust, and to dust you shall return." (Gen 3:19)

But God seeks for you. He knows all your hiding places and all your masks. He knows why you go to that particular behaviour and why you feel comfort in that particular character. He knows how it has changed you and He knows when you first went there. After all of that, He still seeks you. He calls out,

"Where are you?"

---

[12] Rick Warren, *Purpose Driven Life: What On Earth Am I Here For?* (Grand Rapids: Zondervan, 2002) p.186

The rhetorical question is an invitation to allow Him to look upon you; for you to step out from the shadows of guilt and shame and sheepishly try and meet His steadfast gaze upon you. His response? To say your name.

He names you with a name which identifies you; a name which takes off all those masks and replaces that first one. The earliest mask was "shame" now it is "free", then it was "guilt" and now it is "grace". God seeks so that you can, like the child, feel the gaze of the one whose embrace is home and to have the one who first named you to address you.

Yes, the Kingdom of God, is like a game of 'hide and seek' where we hide and where an all-knowing Father seeks. He never gives up on the game but will continue to allow you to remain hidden but will wait for you to reveal yourself to Him and allow Him to gaze upon you and to know you, as if for the first time. He waits for you to step out from your hiding place, which you have chosen, and invites you to make Him your hiding place. He is the only mask that you need to wear. He is the only hiding place you need. Your identity, you name, is found in Him.

But the Kingdom of God is also like a game of 'hide and seek' because there are times when we feel like God is hiding. Where the separation between us and God is not our own choice. We repent; we turn back only to find His presence is not felt. His love feels absent. This experience of remaining in the dark; alone, when it occurs, it feels as if you are the first and only person to ever have felt it. That which you had experienced now gone or has become a faded memory. Was He real when you held each other close? Or was it a dream?

But it's all part of the game.

I love a good puzzle; the thrill of an unanswered question, a fascination with links, connections, series of events, cause and effect. I love a good detective story; Sherlock Holmes, Batman (the original DC), Jonathan Creek. So, what is it about ordained ministry that enthuses me? The love of theology; that wrestling with the ultimate unanswered question: God.

I seek Him. I search for Him. I try to answer Him. It's all part of the game. Where is He? Where will I find Him? When will He appear? The pain of separation still marks me, like everyone else but I try to remind myself in the darkest most challenging times, it's part of the game.

As a minister, speaking in these terms can come across heartless and distant. For the experience isn't 'fun'. Being the 'seeker' is hard and, at times, impossible. Like a child, we try everywhere and yet the person we seek remains absent. As a child, you begin to ask the question,

"What if I never find Him?"

For someone going through the search, it is anything but a game but the search is a daily task and so it becomes a dance. A dance which involves others. Their moves, responses, choices, all contributing to the relationship, another part of the sequence all adding up to an infinitely complex matrix of God and His creation. It's the part of the game where you call for help.

"Mama, Papa is not in the bed and I told him to hide there while I counted to ten."

The study and search for God, eternal and distinct from creation can only be done through the clues He leaves. All of them exist in reality, our day to day lives, they're just not always as they seem. His fingerprints hidden from the careless glance.

When seeking, you become aware of the need to be systematic; it's no good frantically throwing things around. In the turmoil of this form of looking you miss the clues of the hiding place. In the noise and clamour of searching you can forget to listen.

When the search becomes too difficult and we verge on giving up, He calls. He speaks our name from behind the veil. If we are not quiet and still we would miss it but it is clear and distinct. The call does not always immediately reveal the hiding place but it brings you closer. In the midst of the separation, when everything is heavy and fruitless, it is easy to believe the lies we tell ourselves,

"He is not here. He is gone."

His call reminds us that He has not gone. At these times it is important to stand still. Stop and wait. Watch. It is in the staying put that we know where to move and when. He wants to be found but do we want to find him? Do we want to be reminded of our need for Him? Are we willing, in His presence to be reminded that we are not who we tell ourselves we are?

Do we want to be reminded that we are dust....

Stability

The meaning of stability: God is not everywhere[13]

The commonly known vows of the Evangelical Council to 'poverty, chastity and obedience' are not explicit in the Rule of St. Benedict, a document which is accepted as one of the key foundational texts of monasticism, but the seed for these vows can be seen in St. Benedict's description of the admission of a new monk into a community. The brother (as described in the Rule) enters the oratory before the other members of the community and God and commits to 'stability, amendment of life, and obedience'[14].

Stability is about faithfulness (chastity), commitment in and to relationships. In a culture where individual freedom is increasingly the central tenet, stability is one of the key ways one can live a counter cultural life. Committing to another person or people and persevering, 'no matter what', comes with the baggage of historical examples of cults, abusive relationships, etc. and so is shied away from most or is seen negatively by more. Relationships are still seen as good things just not at the cost of personal freedom.

Our society has a big problem with relationships. Different socio-political and philosophical understanding of social interaction, their purpose and shape, confuses the whole topic of how we relate. How Scripture describes loving fellowship and covenants is very different to our modern view of more contractual, secular relationships. Add to that the capitalist, consumer, neo-liberal and liberal political philosophy into the mix and it is no

---

[13] Meister Eckhart in Dwight Longenecker, *St Benedict and St Thérèse: the little rule and the little way* (Herefordshire: Gracewing, 2002) p.96

[14] RB 58:17 in Owen Chadwick (trans.), *The Library of Christian Classics Vol. XII: Western Asceticism* (London: SCM Press Ltd., 1958) p.328

surprise that marriage and sexuality are such explosive conversations. I want to argue that rediscovering the explicit commitment to stability based on a theology of creation outlined in the previous chapter leads to a more sustainable and disciplined life in community.

The English Benedictines released a very good video outlining the life of Benedictine monks. In the video, Dom. Alexander Bevan discussed stability. He said,

> In the first place, monastic consecration involves 'stability'; persevering in the monastic life in a particular community. Stability, here, is connected to the people rather than to the place.[15]

This commitment to others, persevering with them despite pain and heartache, is picked up by Brian C. Taylor. On stability, he writes,

> The Benedictine vow of stability is a vow to a community of people… In this sense it is a marriage…The grass is not greener "over there": one must work out one's problems with *this* person because, if one doesn't, one will have to work it out with *that* person. This is precisely what is so freeing about the vow of stability, both in monastic life and family life. To have to work it out is to demand growth, as painful as it is, and that is freeing. Faithfulness is a limit that forces us to stop running and encounter God, self, and other right now, right here.[16]

---

[15] Dom. Alexander Bevan, *To Prefer Nothing to Christ Part 1 - Consecration, English Benedictines*, https://vimeo.com/153230237

[16] Brian C. Taylor, *Spirituality For Everyday Living: an adaptation of the rule of St. Benedict* (Minnesota: The Liturgical Press, 1989) p.17)

One of the painful frustrations I have had, personally, is the seemingly conflicting calls on my life. I made a commitment to my wife by getting married to her; a vow I made with eagerness and intention (and I was thankful every day that I did.) Before her death, I struggled with that commitment and my call to live a monastic life. I have also made a commitment to serve God's Church by taking on holy orders and embracing, in my case, a priestly role within God's Church within the parochial system of the Church of England (again I'm thankful, most days, that I did.) This, too, jars with my sense of vocation to enter the devoted life. I would like to argue, however, that these two commitments help me to grow in my understanding and engagement in the monastic vows.

There is some richness in referring to a married partner as 'the ball and chain' because on a spiritual level that is what they are. Being bound to that person with no escape route is what gives the freedom outlined above. Yes, lifetime commitments are incredibly risky; rife with potential pain and abuse. I don't want to paint married life as some glorious romp through a fantasy; rather the complete opposite. There is an overly romantic vision of marriage, which, although no one admits to agreeing with, still shapes many of our expectations.

I have been a part of countless weddings through my ministry and most have been with young couples. I often ask these couples, many who have children and live together what made them decide to get married. There is a sense, underlying their responses, of wanting something more from their relationship. The first buds of excitement and infatuation have faded into a kind of mundane existence and marriage is either seen as an expectation or naming of this new state or a booster shot to by-gone days. As well as this, however, there is often the unspoken, unarticulated desire for something more stable and permanent, be that purely legal or the much more enriching emotional stability that comes from such commitment.

I am often reminded of the advice given to Pelagia by her father, Dr. Iannis in Louis de Bernières' book, 'Captain Corelli's Mandolin',

> Love is a temporary madness, it erupts like volcanoes and then subsides. And when it subsides you have to make a decision. You have to work out whether your roots have so entwined together that it is inconceivable that you should ever part. Because this is what love is. Love is not breathlessness, it is not excitement, it is not promulgation of promises of eternal passion, it is not the desire to mate every second minute of the day, it is not lying awake at night imagining that he is kissing every cranny of your body. No, don't blush, I am telling you some truths. That is just being "in love", which any fool can do. Love itself is what is left over when being in love has burned away... Your mother and I had it, we had roots that grew towards each other underground, and when all the pretty blossom had fallen from our branches we found that we were one tree and not two.[17]

Dr Iannis goes on to say,

> Imagine giving up your home and your people, only to discover after six months, a year, three years, that the trees have had no roots and have fallen over. Imagine the desolation. Imagine the imprisonment.[18]

Although this advice holds certain beautiful truths within it, de Bernières' description of how 'love', as opposed to being 'in love', happens remains slightly too idealistic for me. This 'entwining' of roots, for de Bernières, is described as a 'both an art and a fortunate

---

[17] Louis de Bernières, *Captain Corelli's Mandolin* (London: Vintage, 1998) p. 345
[18] ibid.

accident'. What de Bernières means by 'an art' we cannot be certain due to difference emphases that can be placed on that word. The addition of the phrase 'fortunate accident', however, seems to betray his, and the wider culture's, deep desire for love to be 'written in the stars'. There is this Disney-fied notion that we are made for each other; that it is Destiny which pairs people up. Reality does not live up to these high expectations not to mention the devastating burden it places on long-term single people. The pressure to find 'the one', 'Mr./Miss Right' is overwhelming!

This romanticized view of love drives many people to make life commitments hoping that Fate will keep them together or, if there is a sense of what de Bernières describes, a willingness to hold out for the 'fortunate accident' of entwined roots. De Bernières gives no advice to the real couples that have no sense of entwined roots and their marriage feels like a 'desolation' and a form of 'imprisonment'.

> …so many people find themselves in the situation of enclosure, in a marriage or a career,… that by their refusal to accept it it has become a trap from which they long to escape, perhaps actually running away, perhaps by resorting to the daydreaming, which begins with that insidious little phrase 'if only…' Family life which is boring, a marriage which has grown stale, an office job which has become deadening are only too familiar.[19]

Dietrich Bonhoeffer's sermon written from his prison cell in May 1943 for the occasion of his niece's wedding is a solid, theological piece on the subject of marriage and it is one that I paraphrase for each wedding that I speak at. At the heart of the sermon is a pithy quote that sums up the difference between the current view of relationships and marriage and that of more traditional Christian view. He writes, 'It is not your love that

[19] de Waal, *Seeking God*, p.59

upholds marriage, but from now on it is marriage that upholds your love.'[20]

The marriage vows, like the monastic vow of stability, should present a radical challenge to our disposable lifestyle where if something seems to be broken, we throw it away and replace it. Stability within relationships is aided, not by an idyllic notion of Destiny that makes us mere pawns in some cosmic game of matchmaking, but rather explicitly acknowledging we are creative agents in all our relationships. The 'success' of a relationship is ours to make and the 'failure' is not the fault of Fate. Bonhoeffer writes directly to the bride and groom (Eberhard) in his wedding sermon,

> It is not good to speak here all too quickly and submissively of God's will and guidance. It is first of all, simply and unmistakably, your thoroughly human will that is at work and celebrates its triumph here…What you have done and do is first and foremost not something pious but something thoroughly of this world. This is why you yourselves and you alone carry the responsibility for it, a responsibility that no one can take from you. More precisely, you, Eberhard, have been given the entire responsibility for the success of your undertaking, with all the happiness that such a responsibility entails.[21]

Stanley Hauerwas articulates the irony of our current romanticism that underpins our culture's view of relationships, be they sexual or communal,

> The irony is that romanticism, which began as an attempt to recapture the power of intimate relation as opposed to the "formal" or institutionalized relationship implied by

[20] Dietrich Bonhoeffer, *Letters and Papers from Prison* (Minneapolis: Fortress Press, 2009) p.84

[21] Ibid., p.82

> marriage, now finds itself recommending the development of people who are actually incapable of sustaining intimate relationships. For intimacy depends on the willingness to give of the self, to place oneself in the hands of another, to be vulnerable, even if that means we may be hurt… I suspect that part of the reason the church has always assumed that marriage is a reality that is prior to love is that genuine love is so capable of destruction that we need a structure to sustain us through the pain and joy of it.[22]

When we experience the sensation of 'imprisonment' or 'enclosure', vows to stability, made to another, helps us to embrace reality rather than flee to a fictitious alternative. As an artist, I have discovered the counter-intuitive truth that limitation brings more satisfying creativity than total liberation and freedom of choice. Creativity is often seen as a 'mystical' event where the artist 'creates only that which the Muse dictates.'[23] There has been a long held mistaken view of the creative process that, like the romantic view of 'love', makes human beings passive partners to some transcendent will, divorced from reality. Robert Sternberg and Todd Lubart, as they wrote in their research on the creative process, portrayed this view in the following terms,

> The creative person was seen as an empty vessel that a divine being would fill with inspiration. The individual would then pour out the inspired ideas, forming an otherworldly product.[24]

---

[22] Stanley Hauerwas, *A Community of Character: toward a constructive Christian social ethic* (Notre Dame: Notre Dame Press, 1981) p.181

[23] Robert Sternberg and Todd Lubart, "The Concept of Creativity: Prospects and Paradigms", Robert Sterberg (ed.), *The Handbook of Creativity* (Cambridge: Cambridge University Press, 1999) p.5

[24] Ibid.

My own experience, and the experience of many other artists, is more akin to the American painter and photographer, Chuck Close, who is famous for saying,

> The advice I like to give young artists, or really anybody who'll listen to me, is not to wait around for inspiration. Inspiration is for amateurs; the rest of us just show up and get to work. If you wait around for the clouds to part and a bolt of lightning to strike you in the brain, you are not going to make an awful lot of work. All the best ideas come out of the process; they come out of the work itself.[25]

The vow to stability is the intentional choice to put down roots and to direct those roots to others. In this way the 'love' described by de Bernières is in no way a 'fortunate accident' but a guaranteed result of a conscious effort of our own resolve. This commitment leads us away from passive agency in some wish fulfilment towards a creative, active engagement in reality.

> For stability says there must be no evasion; instead attend to the real, to the real necessity however uncomfortable that might be. Stability brings us from a feeling of alienation, perhaps from the escape into fantasy and daydreaming, into the state of reality. It will not allow us to evade the inner truth of whatever it is that we have to do, however dreary and boring and apparently unfruitful that may seem. It involves listening…to the particular demands of whatever this task and this moment in time is asking; no more and no less. This is the limitation which

[25] Chuck Close in Paul Klein, *The Art Rules: wisdom and guidance from artworld experts* (Bristol: Intellect, 2015) p120

> the artist knows when he accepts the necessity imposed upon him and turns it to good.[26]

Above all, this embracing of the reality of relationship and the intentional refusal to look for something better elsewhere reveals the true autonomy within us rather than excusing ourselves from blame by looking to an outside agent, however benevolent! In a consumer culture, which is built on the primacy of 'choice', stability seems to be, in one sense, the antithesis, a restriction of choice. If we look closer, however, at how the notion of choice is used within our commercial society we soon discover that the constant questioning of one's choices undermines the potency of the choices we make. In one moment we choose a particular pair of trainers and immediately after the culture requires us to feel 'lack' and question the choice we made. The perpetuation of our culture requires us never to find satisfaction in our choices thus leading us to continue to choose alternative consumables. Choices, therefore, can never fully be made because we are immune from the consequences or impact of those choices.

Stability, as with all commitment, is not anti-choice but rather pro-choice[27] for it still requires of us to use our freedom of choice but, unlike consumerism, to feel the full weight of our decisive action. We become, through our vows of stability, more aware of the reality of our free-will for better and for worse. It requires us to, like Adam and Eve, to grasp our freedom, the gift of God, and to boldly use it; what it requires, however, is wisdom as to how we do it. That is why, in the marriage service, the couple are reminded that they are not to use their freedom of choice 'lightly or selfishly but reverently and responsibly'[28]. Committing to something or someone also require a daily use of our free-will to keep persevering and not to strip ourselves of the power to decide.

---

[26] de Waal, *Seeking God*, p. 60

[27] This is not to be interpreted as any comment on abortion.

[28] The Archbishops' Council, *Common Worship: Pastoral Services* (London: Church House Publishing, 2005) p.105

Within the environment of stability, we also discover a deeper humility when it comes to knowing our own identity. As we explored in the previous chapter, we put on masks to define us out of fear that people may see what we really are: confused, indecisive and lost children. In the age of identity politics, we talk of our 'true selves' as static and primordial but, again, we approach the topic of identity as passive recipients as though we play no part in the creation of our identities. We grasp hold of any definition we have, that which separates and distinguishes from others as an attempt to show that we can use the power of our freedom. We are told that we are free and yet, when it comes to selfhood, we want to ascribe to an unchangeable identity. We look around ourselves and we believe we see everyone with the answer to that deepest of questions: who am I?

Polonius' advice to his son Laertes in Hamlet Act 1 scene iii, "to thine own self be true."[29] has been used by many to mean one must try and know ones 'true' self and develop it.[30] The phrase was picked up and explored by Henrik Ibsen in Peer Gynt[31] as the protagonist sets out on a journey of self-discovery. Ibsen's play is an exploration of the human need for self-understanding and our deeply held belief that we are masters of our own destiny. In Peer's struggle we see our own struggle. Esther de Waal writes,

> Everyone needs to feel at home to feel earthed, for it is impossible to say, 'Who am I?' without first asking, 'Where am I? Whence have I come? Where am I going?' Without roots we can neither discover where we belong,

---

[29] William Shakespeare, *Hamlet* ()p.

[30] Scholars would argue that Elizabethian thought suggests this advice is more about self interest, i.e. look after your own affairs in order that you can look after others, and not about self identity.

[31] Henrik Ibsen, Kenneth McLeish (trans.), *Peer Gynt* (London: Nick Hern Books, 1999) p.45

> nor can we grow… Without stability we cannot know our true selves.[32]

This is the irony we face: in our desire for the next best thing, keeping our options open and never settling on any choice, we are unable to truly discover who we are divorced from the cultural demands and free from how the world and others are shaping us. In our constant state of seeking we are also franticly searching for an anchor to hold us steady in the dizzying reality of life we create. In order to survive this emotional torment we create, in our minds, seemingly unmovable identities to cling hold to not realizing they are lies of our own making.

The play Peer Gynt ends with the protagonist realizing that true selfhood is an impossible dream and discovers that one is only truly found in the love of another, i.e. he is defined by how another sees him in love. Peer Gynt meets The Button Moulder who requires Peer to be melted down and recreated because he hasn't really lived a life of any consequence (his choices were never allowed to make an impact).

"You've been self-ish but not yourself." Then the Button Moulder has this passing comment about how one is true to one's self, "To be yourself is to destroy your Self." Thomas Merton, a 20th century Trappist monk, had a lot to say about self-identity and, like the Button Moulder in Peer Gynt, he suggests,

> In order to become myself I must cease to be what I always thought I wanted to be, and in order to find myself I must go out of myself, and in order to live I have to die. The reason for this is that I am born in selfishness and therefore my natural efforts to make myself more real and

---

[32] de Waal, *Seeking God*, p.56

> more myself, make me less real and less myself because they revolve around a lie.[33]

We must stop seeking self-definitions but allow ourselves to be defined by others, vulnerable and dangerous as that may be. Stability invites us into the reality that we are who/what we spend time with. Despite being such social beings, however, defined as we are by others, our shame and fear of abandonment, of isolation, ironically forces us to live in our self-made lie and not allow others into our inner world. We strongly assert our desired identity as a subconscious means of protecting ourselves from experiencing the shame of discovery. Once we have settled into a tribe who accept our presented self, we face another issue: our identities are so intrinsically linked to the tribe or community where we experience belonging that it is hard to acknowledge, let alone experience, change.

> Without this ultimate commitment to the other monks, to wife or husband, to child or parent, change is difficult at best because it lives under the threat of abandonment. With a commitment to stability, change is no longer a threat but something to be undertaken together. One can change or ask for change in the other when one knows that one is loved and that this request will not drive the other away.[34]

The denial and rejection of abandonment itself within a relationship liberates us from the need to present a strong self-knowledge and we can allow ourselves to accept the change people can make to us. The gaze of a beloved, be it a spouse, a friend, a child lures us into the vulnerable act of stripping back the masks. We are able, within a committed, trusting, long-term relationship,

---

[33] Thomas Merton, *New Seeds of Contemplation* (New York: New Directions, 1972) p. 47
[34] Taylor, *Spirituality For Everyday Living*, p.17-18

to say, "All I know is I am dust but dust that is loved by this other person."

For Peer, Solveig, the woman who has loved him despite his infamous flaws, is that 'other'. The final moments of Ibsen's play sees Peer asking Solveig to define him in order to save him from being melted down,

> Peer: …Where has Peer Gynt been?
> Solveig: Been?
> Peer: Yes! … Since he sprang from the mind of God. Can you answer?…
> Solveig: The answer's easy.
> Peer: You know? Where I've been? Myself, entire, complete – Peer Gynt, with God's stamp on my brow?
> Solveig: In my faith. In my hope. In my love.
> Peer: What? Your love? In your love? Myself exists in that?… Hide me, then, oh hide me in your love![35]

Solveig's response to Peer is cryptic and poetic. Many scholars have explored what Ibsen might mean by 'In my faith. In my hope. In my love.' Most agree that it is an expression of a type of generous 'seeing'. Solveig views Peer's life, as it develops over time, as a patchwork of action and intention. She has faith; because she sees a different narrative being told through Peer's life; a story, which he has missed. Solveig has hope; because she knows Peer has the potential to be something other than he thinks he is. Solveig loves Peer not because of what he has done, or what he says but loves him for the man he could be if he made the choice to. This is at the heart of what Christian's understanding of love is. Esther de Waal writes,

> Genuine love is free from exploitation or the manipulation of others. Where this is missing love becomes a delusion,

---

[35] Ibsen, *Peer Gynt*, p.131

> a subterfuge, a means to an end. The patience and gentleness … are again virtues which Benedict admires and which he has been encouraging. This is the opposite of that violence which is not limited to aggressive behaviour but may be a reflection of the hidden violence of feelings which comes out in tone of voice or the glance… The 'wicked zeal of bitterness' must refer to the rivalries and power games that can tear communities apart, the sort of competition that is unsuitable in the body of Christ. If you must compete, he seems to say, at least compete in love![36]

Stability, rooted and grounded in the story of true love, shapes our thinking and moves to correct our emotional response to others and the world in which we live. This form of 'genuine' love is not natural to us and takes practice and like most practice it is difficult at first, tempting us to give up, but in persevering we grow and develop outside what we were capable of before. To affirm an objective story, ie. a story that can be shared, is a direct challenge to the liberal, postmodern philosophy which is so subjective and individualistic.

Relationships, as we all have experienced, are fragile and uncertain. The other person is not stable or pure; they too misuse their free-will in ways that will impact us in negative and hurtful ways. We cannot be sure whether the way they see us is real or whether they are seeing what we want them to see. There is still, within these committed relationships the high risk of emotional abandonment if not physical. How do we protect ourselves from the pain?

Thomas Merton concludes,

> …there is only one problem on which all my existence, my peace and my happiness depend: to discover myself in

[36] Esther de Waal, *A Life Giving Way: a commentary on the Rule of St. Benedict* (London: Continuum, 1995) p.211

> discovering God. If I find Him I will find myself and if I find my true self I will find Him. But although this looks simple, it is in reality immensely difficult… The only One who can teach me to find God is God, Himself, Alone.[37]

In Galatians, Paul writes,

> For freedom Christ has set us free. Stand firm, therefore, and do not submit again to a yoke of slavery…For you were called to freedom, brothers and sisters; only do not use your freedom as an opportunity for self-indulgence, but through love become slaves to one another. For the whole law is summed up in a single commandment, "You shall love your neighbour as yourself." If, however, you bite and devour one another, take care that you are not consumed by one another. (Gal 5:1, 13-15)

Plato, in his book 'Republic', depicts democracy as a denigration of strong governance and places the democratic regime just above tyranny. The democratic man, which he uses to portray the character of democracy, is a man who is free to do what they want and live how they want. This democratic man is ruled by his passions and base desires. He is uneducated with little self-control. Democracy is painted as self-autonomous units fighting and competing to survive. Stanley Hauerwas agrees,

> The problem with our society is not that democracy has not worked, but that it has… We have been freed to pursue happiness and "every citizen has been granted the desired freedom and material goods in such quantity and of such quality as to guarantee in theory the achievement of happiness… the constant desire to have still more things

[37] Merton, *New Seeds of Contemplation*, p. 36

> and still better life and the struggle to obtain them imprints many Western faces with worry and even depression."[38] [39]

At the time of writing the world is experiencing a significant increase in violent rhetoric and protest. Western culture is increasingly polarized and communities are crumbling over sexual, racial and gender politics. I would argue it is because we no longer have a shared narrative to our lives together. The removal of the need to discover, together, a shared identity or, to put it another way, the need to remove a forced shared identity has led to the erosion of family, community and fellowship and to the high levels of loneliness, mental health issues, depression, anxiety and violence; and it is that one word which describes the tone of political debate: 'violence'.

Are we surprised that, despite a culture that espouses tolerance, we find ourselves more opposed to others?

> Liberalism is successful exactly because it supplies us with a myth that seems to make sense of our social origins… A people do not need a shared history; all they need is a system of rules that will constitute procedures for resolving disputes as they pursue their various interests.[40]

Hauerwas' criticism of, specifically American, liberal democracy raises the important issue of freedom of choice within a social context.

> The great ironies of our society is that by attempting to make freedom an end in itself we have become an excessively legalistic society… there is no need for

---

[38] Alexander Solzhenitsyn, an address given at Harvard University, Harvard Gazette, June 1978, p.1

[39] Hauerwas, *Community of Character*, p.75

[40] Ibid., p.78

> voluntary self-restraint, as we are free to operate to the limit of the law.[41]

Again we see that by promoting liberation of the self we actually place more severe limitations upon us. As we have become more aware of the limitations that such an individualized society demands, frenetic attempts to respond without changing direction leads to increasing violence. Violence is rooted in fear. Violence is the response to when our worldview and view of self feels threatened. Violence is characterised by the cross as we respond to the shock of seeing, in the presence of God's love for us, the reality of our lives for the first time. In an attempt to make sense of the dissonance brought about by Jesus we reject our own reality in favour of the daydream we've built around ourselves.

> …"in the public theatre, differences arise only to fall; each new difference has a limitless ambition to obliterate all others, and therefore to cancel out difference itself."[42] The best a secular peace can hope for, then, is a "tolerable" regulation or management of conflict by one coercive means or another.[43]

'The most coercive aspect of the liberal account of the world,' argues Hauerwas, 'is that we are free to make up our own story.'[44] This is why it is so important, as we seek a theological framework for the sustainable life of community, we must start with our shared, a-contextual story. We must be a people rooted together in one story. It is only from that grounding that we can truly grow, together.

---

[41] Ibid., p.75

[42] John Milbank, *Theology and Social Theory: beyond secular reason* (Massachusetts: Blackwell Publishing, 2006) p.290-291)

[43] Stanley Hauerwas, *Performing the Faith: Bonhoeffer and the practice of nonviolence* (London: SPCK, 2004) p.88

[44] Ibid., p.84

So, what should our response be in the world we currently inhabit? How does the vow of stability aid us in our common life? It is only by remaining rooted in the story of God that we can bear with one another in love; not the love that allows people to live how they want but the love which desires that people belong and are brought together. This love is not merely allowing others to exist nearby but an intentional desire for transformation and growth. This love is rooted in the monastic vow of stability, ongoing conversion and obedience.

This resolution, within the Christian narrative, to stand firm and be formed in a particular place by particular people is to learn to see 'the world not as a given but as truly a gift from God'

> A better way to describe Christian ethics, then, is not as a choosing or deciding what is the right thing to do but being educated in the art of rightly accepting gifts.[45]

We are to use the gift of freedom to acknowledge and to accept the authority of God and to allow His eternal gaze of love to form and shape us, to define us. In this way we aren't looking to create democratic Christian communities because 'the church is radically not democratic if by democratic we mean that no one knows the truth and therefore everyone's opinion counts equally.'[46] The only way we walk into a more social politic is by embracing authority, not in society, nor in an individual but in God.[47] The only view that is trustworthy and true is the one who is able to oversee the whole story, the one who can exist outside of the narrative itself. We are blessed, however, that the narrator has stepped into the story to direct and lead us.

We are called to embed ourselves solely in the reality of the love of God, revealed in the person of Jesus Christ and taught to us

---

[45] Ibid., p.92
[46] Hauerwas, *A Community of Character*, p.85
[47] Ibid., p.84

through the lives of the saints, which provokes us to see ourselves and others not as different in gender, sexuality, race or class but as equal under the authority of God. We are to receive our identity in Him and Him alone. In this way we no longer need to fear abandonment or rejection of others because our roots are entwined with the one who gives us life and brings us to our true self. The outward facts of ourselves, our bodies, colouring, geography, etc. are the context in which we exist but we are to use our freedom to choose to be known through God. In this place of trust we can then commit to other people in relationship because 'at the heart of stability is the certitude that God is everywhere, that we have no need to seek God elsewhere, that if I can't find God here I shan't find Him anywhere.'[48]

In the Conferences of Cassian, Abba Piamun, a Desert Father, discusses three types of monks that have developed over the monastic tradition. He names the types of monks as cenobites (coenobites), hermits and sarabaites. Cenobites are 'monks living in a community under the government of a single elder.' Hermits are 'men who have first been trained in communities to the life of virtue and have then chosen to live a completely hidden and solitary life.' Sarabaites, however, do not come out well.

> The third, and culpable, kind is the Sarabaites… They are descended from Ananias and Sapphira. They do not follow the perfect way: they prefer to pretend to follow it. No doubt they want to be rivals of, and to gain the kind of credit given to, people who choose Christ's utter poverty above all the riches of the world. They pursue true goodness feebly. They must needs become monks in order to gain the repute of monks, but they make no effort to follow their discipline, disregard the rules of the communities, are outside all control from the elders, fail to

[48] Metropolitan Anthony Bloom quoted in de Waal, *Seeking God*, p.62

> use the elders' traditions to conquer their self-will. They... go on living in their homes just as before, carrying on the same work; or they build cells for themselves, call them 'monasteries' and live in them as they please... Shirking the austere rule of a community: living two or three together in a cell; under no direction: aiming above all else at having freedom from the elders, of going where they like, and of satisfying whatever passion they like – they are more busied about the necessities of life day and night than are coenobites.[49]

St. Benedict's treatment of the Sarabaites gives the same cutting critique.

> ...unschooled by any rule, untested, as gold is by fire, but soft as lead, living in and of the world... They live together in twos or threes, more often alone, without a shepherd in their own fold, not the Lord's. Their only law is the pleasure of their desires, and whatever they wish or choose they call holy. They consider whatever they dislike unlawful. [50]

Critics of the New Monastic movement are right in holding these excerpts as a mirror on those of us who are exploring this emerging vocation. We, who are undertaking discernment to what God might be doing within his Church, must take these dangers seriously and face up to the wisdom found within them. We must, therefore, take seriously the vows to stability (which leads to obedience) within our community life. It is this criticism that gives me greatest pause when considering the rising use of monastic terms, such as 'Rule of Life', to describe personal aspirations

---

[49] Cassian, The Conferences of Cassian, "Conference 18: Conference of Abba Piamun on the three sorts of monks", Owen Chadwick (trans.), *Library of Christian Classics Volume XII: Western Asceticism* (London: SCM Press, 1958) p.268-269
[50] RB 1:7-9

without formal commitment to others and accountability or discipline.

St. Benedict also describes a fourth kind of monk: the gyratory monks.

> All their lives they wander in different countries staying in various monasteries for three or four days at a time. They are restless, servants to the seduction of their own will and appetites, and are much worse in all things than the Sarabaites.[51]

The distinction, it seems, between Sarabaites and gyratory monks is the travelling. They move around and don't remain rooted in one place. They are nomads with no security from which to grow. Some within the New Monastic movement have developed an understanding based more on friars rather than monks. The friars, or mendicants, adopt more of a travelling, itinerant ministry visiting, particularly urban areas preaching, evangelising and ministering, especially to the poor. The mendicant orders still have a Rule and an abbot figure called by various names depending on the different orders. The mendicants were released from the traditional lifetime interpretation of the Benedictine vow to stability giving them freedom to roam and preach where need is found.

> The emergence of urban centers meant concentrated numbers of the homeless and the sick. This created problems for the parish churches who found themselves unable to address these issues. In response to this crisis, there emerged the new mendicant orders founded by Francis of Assisi (c.1181-1226) and Dominic of Guzmán (c.1170-1234).[52]

---

[51] RB 1:10-11

[52] "The Mendicant Orders", University of Saint Thomas–Saint Paul, Minnesota, 2003, http://courseweb.stthomas.edu/medieval/francis/mendicant.html

They remain though, deeply committed to those that they minister to and are in relationship with those they minister alongside. Stability (or 'chastity') is still a principle to which they aspire and seek out in their lives and in their relationship. Their travelling is not in search of something nor is it escaping something else; they move under the obedience of shared sense of call. We, who are still immature in the discipline of religious life, must be more wary of mis-interpreting the slight distinction between being obedient to a discernment of God's Spirit and our own deep-seated desire to flee from the difficulties of relationship. Nor should we place upon us a lifetime commitment to a place if it is not God's will for us to do so. It is in the tension of these two calls that I sense God revealing a new order that balances the prayerful, devoted monastics and the more overtly missional, serving mendicant. Is it in this between place that we may find a deep sense of the Christian disciple as a 'tent-dweller', both rooted and stable and yet nomadic?

These conversations between those who are more mendicant in their vision and vocation and those who are more Benedictine will be rife with misunderstandings and divisions of purpose, but I feel that if we can remain faithful to one another, there is a space that is evolving where all can be of one heart and mind. These conversations must be done with the utmost prayer and sensitivity of the Spirit. There must be a deep commitment throughout the discernment and conversations to faithfulness, an openness to the inner conversion and obedience to the Lord who directs and guides us. Even in these discussions we can model a way of being together which 'exhibit in our common life the kind of community possible when trust, and not fear, rules our lives,'[53] and this will be a gift to the wider Church as all disciples discern when to stay and when to go.

[53] Hauerwas, *A Community of Character*, p. 85

Prayer

Prayer is the central avenue God uses to transform us.[54]

We have explored so far the nature of a true humility required to begin a journey into the communal life of our Trinitarian God; a humility that demands we see ourselves and the reality we live in as it is rather than an ideal we desire. This humility is encouraged when we face others who challenge the narrative we can easily write for ourselves and who force us to discover a wider story for us to inhabit. In order for us to avoid being destroyed or manipulated by the misuse of relationships with other human beings, broken and fallen as we all are, we need to discover an 'other' who can act in genuine love, which does not manipulate or control; that other can only be God Himself.

We now turn to the practices which enable this facing of the Other who, by allowing His gaze to fall on us we find our identity in His love. By being in His presence we are transformed into His likeness. By freely choosing to be in relationship with Him we discover roots that give us stability so we can relate to other people and persevere in community. I will be calling the collective term for these practices 'prayer' but we may also call it worship, adoration and/or devotion. Prayer, in this context, refers to activities which root us in the Divine, which focus our attention on God and through which we intentionally take off the masks, come out of hiding and allow our loving Father to hold us in His reality.

We have seen that temptation to sin, to be separated from God, is built into creation through the gift of free will. We have been given choice in order for our relationship with God to be

[54] Richard Foster, *Celebration Of Discipline: the path to spiritual growth* (London: Hodder & Stoughton, 2008) p.42

genuine. To stop us continually getting lost in the created world and being tempted to take paths that will lead to further isolation and loneliness we must freely choose to submit our choices to God who will guide and help us as we live within His world. In the next chapter we will explore the way in which God collaborates with us in our free will but for now it is enough to state that we must learn afresh to listen to His voice and seek Him while He may be found.

If the life of faith is like a game of hide and seek then we need to find ways to continually return to a form of stillness and quiet to hear for God calling our name from behind the curtain and move closer to Him. Prayer is that action of silencing out the chaotic cacophony of temptations and distractions to intentionally seek a reunion with God. This will involve confession of those things that hide us or have separated us from God and reconciliation in our relationship with Him. It will undoubtedly involve intercession as we invite God to enter into our lives and those for whom we pray on behalf of to bring change. Above all, however, this reunion with God must involve contemplation; intently gazing upon Him who loves us and allowing His love to impact us in our deeper being.

Thomas Merton's excellent book, 'Contemplative Prayer', repeats the idea that 'all our meditation should begin with the realisation of our nothingness and helplessness in the presence of God.'[55]

> There is a "movement" of meditation, expressing the basic "paschal" rhythm of the Christian life, the passage from death to life in Christ. Sometimes prayer, meditation and contemplation are "death" – a kind of descent into our own nothingness, a recognition of helplessness, frustration, infidelity, confusion, ignorance.[56]

---

[55] Thomas Merton, *Contemplative Prayer* (London: Darton, Longman and Todd, 2005) p.86

[56] Ibid., p.40

It is this understanding that contemplation of the Divine begins with an acknowledgement of our own 'nothingness' that places prayer at the start of our discipleship formation. If we skip this stage out of a fear of experiencing crushing low self-esteem or, worse, out of sense that the negative thoughts we have of ourselves are the same thing as this humility before God, then we do not truly 'die to self'. If 'humility is not thinking less of yourself; it is thinking of yourself less'[57] then any usual masochistic self-loathing is not the same as facing our own nothingness, it is rather a negative version of intense egoism in which our identity remains firmly rooted in the illusion that we alone are at centre of the universe.

This journey into the life of God, therefore, begins with that liturgical refrain: 'remember you are dust and to dust you shall return. Turn away from sin and be faithful to Christ.'[58] In this theological statement, in order to repent (turn around) and begin a pilgrimage towards God, we must remember that we are dust. There must be no illusion as to who or what we are. The masks must be removed but (and it is an important 'but') this is done in the presence of the one, who has revealed again and again, His love for you and for the sole purpose of receiving again our true identity in Him. This is where Christian contemplation/meditation is distinct from Eastern religious forms; we do not seek an emptiness as a goal in itself but rather we empty ourselves as we seek to be filled, fully, by the indwelling of Christ by His Holy Spirit.

> …Contemplation is the summit of the Christian life of prayer, for the Lord desires nothing of us so much as to become, himself, our "way", our "truth and life."… No logic of our own can accomplish this transformation of our interior life. We cannot argue that "emptiness" equals "the

[57] Warren, *Purpose Driven Life*, p.186

[58] The Archbishops' Council, *Common Worship: Times and Seasons* (London:Church House Publishing, 2006) p.230

> presence of God" and then sit down to acquire the presence of God by emptying our soul of every image. It is not a matter of logic or of cause and effect. It is not a matter of desire, of planned enterprise, or of our own spiritual technique...An emptiness that is deliberately cultivated, for the sake of fulfilling a personal spiritual ambition, is not empty at all: it is full of itself.[59]

Evagrius of Ponticus, who taught a three-stage process for monks in their development in the spiritual life, starts with a form of 'pure prayer' that is 'the continual intercourse of the spirit with God.'[60] This mirrors the description of prayer described by Charles de Foucauld,

> When one loves one longs to be forever in converse with him one loves, or at least to be always in his sight. Prayer is nothing else. This is what prayer is: intimate intercourse with the Beloved. You look at him; you tell him of your love; you are happy at his feet; you tell him you will live and die there.[61]

Thus this form of 'emptying' prayer is rather an emptying of one thing, ie. ourselves, and an immediate filling with another, ie. God. John of Ruysbroeck, a 13th century Flemish mystic, wrote on this two-fold 'conversation' with God in his book, 'The Adornment of the Spiritual Marriage'.

> At times, the inward man... meets God without intermediary. And from out the Divine Unity, there shines into him a simple light; and this light shows him Darkness and Nakedness and Nothingness... In the Nakedness, he

[59] Merton, *Contemplative Prayer*, p. 117
[60] Evagrius of Ponticus, Prayer, in Robert Edward Sinkewicz, *Evagrius of Ponticus: the Greek ascetic corpus* (New York: Oxford University Press, 2006) p. 192
[61] Charles de Foucauld, *Meditations of a Hermit* (London: Burns & Oates, 1981) p.4

> loses the perception and discernment of all things, and is transfigured and penetrated by a simple light. In the Nothingness, all his activity fails him; for he is vanquished by the working of God's abysmal love, and in the fruitive inclination of his spirit he vanquishes God, and becomes one spirit with him… And he is filled, according to the measure in which he has sunk himself in his essential being, with the abysmal delights and riches of God.[62]

Evagrius' aim, as with most of the Desert Fathers and Mothers, was to achieve a 'purity of heart', 'an unconditional and totally humble surrender to God, a total acceptance of ourselves and of our situation as willed by him.'

> It means the renunciation of all deluded images of ourselves, all exaggerated estimates of our own capacities, in order to obey God's will as it comes to us in the difficult demands of life in its exacting truth. Purity of heart is then a correlative to a new spiritual identity – the "self" as recognized in the context of realities willed by God.[63]

Prayer should place us in the presence of God in the posture of humility. One of the words most translated as 'worship' in the Hebrew Scriptures is שָׁחָה (*shachah*). It means to depress oneself, to bow down, to prostrate oneself on the ground. This pose involves vulnerability as the person who bows down bares their neck to another and chooses to not watch nor defend from an attack from them. In other words, in worship we place ourselves in a lowly position, giving God, the object of worship, full reign to do with us

---

[62] John of Ruysbroeck, C.A. Wynschenk Dom. (trans.), *The Adornment of the Spiritual Marriage: the sparkling stone & the book of supreme truth* (New York: Cosimo Classics, 2007) p.150
[63] Merton, *Contemplative Prayer*, p.83

what He likes with no chance of defense from us (or at least that's the ideal!)

With this understanding it is worth reflecting on the idea of idolatry. We can easily imagine idolatry, when described in the Bible, to mean just bowing down to pictures or statues, which some 'ignorant pagan' believes has some special powers to intervene in their lives. If we consider, however, that an idol is the image of something that we hand our life over to, our choices and the direction of our lives, then idolatry becomes more real to our 21st century lives.

Expanding on the understanding of *shachah* to mean the handing over control of one's life, worship becomes a desire to have our lives shaped in a particular way. We can worship money, substances, a celebrity, an ideology, philosophy or religion. Consumerism, in this framework is a form of worship, as we allow our choices to be made for us by advertisements or the culture of acquisition. Our identity is based on the notion that 'I buy therefore I am', our value is trapped within the products we own; we are possessed by our possessions. Consumerism is the worship of objects, gadgets, stuff.

Celebrity culture is also a form of worship. With certain individuals elevated to the status of 'god' be they sports personalities, fashion icons or 'pop idols'. The way they live impacts how we live as we seek to imitate them. Their thoughts and views can powerfully shape ours. They can transform us as we allow their choices to direct ours. "It is no longer I who live but Taylor Swift."[64] This idolatry of personality is not restricted to famous figures but can be more local in the form of any person we spend time with and look up to.

We return again to the concept of choice and how we intentionally engage our free will. God endowed us with freedom in order to choose; ultimately to choose to be with Him and to be

---

[64] a variation of Gal 2:20: 'It is no longer I who live but Christ.'

shaped by Him. That choice is worship. We are made for worship and if we are not worshipping God then we are worshipping something/someone else. We must begin by identifying those things that we worship and then strip ourselves of these idols. This process is our unmasking in order that we can return to God naked as we were born. Prayer/worship is the continual process of opening ourselves to God, coming out from our hiding place, with the intentional desire to be named by Him afresh.

Shachah is deeply connected with another, similar Hebrew word, שׁוּחַ (*shuach*) which means to humble oneself, to sink or bow down. It is used three times in the Old Testament; once in Proverbs 2:18, once in Lamentations 3:20[65] and Psalm 44,

> Rouse yourself! Why do you sleep, O Lord?
> Awake, do not cast us off forever!
> Why do you hide your face?
> Why do you forget our affliction and oppression?
> For we ***sink down*** to the dust;
> our bodies cling to the ground.
> Rise up, come to our help.
> Redeem us for the sake of your steadfast love. (Ps 44:23-26)

This very physical depiction of worship speaks of an attitude of the heart that we should approach God with but it also speaks of God's approach to us. If we consider the image of a subject kneeling before their sovereign, head bowed and the monarch stretches out their hand to be held by that subject, it can easily be seen as a power play. The subject is vulnerable and cast down, lowly and submissive. The monarch is aloof and dominant but consider that hand, outstretched. It is, in some senses quite a vulnerable thing for a sovereign to do; they are allowing the subject

[65] The King James Version translate shuach as 'humbled', as in, 'My soul hath them still in remembrance, and is humbled in me.'

to hold onto them. It would be easy for the subject to pull them down and do them great damage. The act of reaching out to the lowly subject has the potential to cost the ruler dearly.

We can approach prayer with the same blind spot. Prayer can easily seem like us stooping, hands wringing and groveling into God's presence for a scrap of His time or attention. It can feel like we are mumbling some request in the vague hope that He may consider us worthy to be heard. The truth is that God reaches out to us. God stoops down into our life to hold us and have us hold Him. Unlike the other idols in our lives, God desires relationship with us and to be impacted by us and He wants to be involved in our lives daily, moment by moment.

This is why daily prayer is so important. It is not just us showing God our dedication and worship of Him; it is equally taking the opportunity for Him to show us His commitment and faithfulness to us. In this way, regularly engaging in prayer practices is a physical outworking of the stability that is required in the life of discipleship. It is in adopting a rhythm of prayer that we find the necessary anchor in our life in the world. This rhythm of prayer must be discovered as the treasure it is and not imposed as a duty it can become.

When I was at college we said Morning Prayer everyday from Monday to Friday at 8.30am. For many of us this was not an ideal time and the form was not to our liking. We were sat down early on by the then warden and she laid down the law. Everyone was expected to come to Morning Prayer, she informed us, unless there were extreme circumstances and ones that had been checked by a tutor. Why? Because it was about setting a habit which would sustain you. It was about developing a prayer life, which wasn't based on how you felt but on commitment to God.

We are so keen to keep relationships on our terms. We know that we are social creatures but we fail, so often, on those demands of real connection. We want partners and friends who fit into our lives but we are not always willing to adapt to fit into theirs.

Relationships need to be mutual if they are to be sustainable. Prayer, therefore, can't be just when we want/need it; there needs to be an element of sitting in God's presence for Him.

> As long as we look for 'interesting experiences' in prayer, we avoid the encounter with God that comes in the midst of our ordinariness. God is beyond illusions and attractive signs. And so sometimes when we sit, not expecting anything, often in boredom, we allow ourselves to settle into the reality of what is, rather than what it is we would like. This is, I feel, the heart of prayer in the form of the offices or any other daily discipline of regular prayer: to settle into our ordinary life in God to the extent that we find a quiet peace there and cease to run after illusory idols.[66]

The New Monastic Movement is encouraging the Church to rediscover this approach to prayer. It is the rhythm of stepping into God's presence, not to just give a list of desires or wants, treating God like a cosmic Santa Claus, but being open to the transformative relationship with the Divine. We become what we spend time with and so if we truly want to be transformed into the likeness of Christ then we need to spend time turning from the idols we are possessed by and encountering our heavenly Father's gaze which re-shapes us. When presented in this way we grasp afresh that 'prayer comes readily and un-self-consciously to one who does his best to implement the teachings of the Gospel in concrete behavior. The monk seeks God, not "experiences".'[67]

It has always been the work of the monastic to dedicate themselves to prayer, not only for themselves but for the wider Kingdom of God. The other word often translated to 'worship' in the Hebrew Scriptures is עָבַד (*avad*) which is also translated as

---

[66] Taylor, *Spirituality for Everyday Living,* p.36

[67] Michael Casey, "St Benedict's Approach to Prayer", *Cistercian Studies* (1980) p.328

'work/service'. It is worth briefly exploring the interplay between these two translations in the Book of Exodus in order for us to understand the vocation of the monastic tradition and how it might impact the wider Church.

In Exodus 4:22-23 God tells Moses to go to Pharaoh and say, "Israel is my firstborn son. I said to you, "Let my son go that he may worship me." But you refused to let him go; now I will kill your firstborn son."" The word used here for worship is *avad.* When Moses goes to Pharaoh and requests this time of worship, Pharaoh refuses and commands "heavier work be laid on them." The word used here for work is *avodah*[68]. When the Israelites ask to go and worship/work with God the Pharaoh demands that they stay and work/worship him instead.

When Thomas Merton suggests, 'the monk is not defined by his task, his usefulness. In a certain sense he is supposed to be 'useless' because his mission is not to do this or that job but to be a man of God'[69] he is articulating that call to be a man (or woman) who gives themselves totally to the will of God. Prayer is work but it is not a task. It is work in the sense that it is to be engaged with intentionally and by our deliberate choice but it may be better to describe it as an attitude by which all other tasks are defined.

> Prayer is not in competition with other activities, and growth in prayer will not be encouraged by the withdrawal from other work if our intention is that every action should be directed towards God.[70]

At the heart of the New Monastic Movement is a call on ordinary disciples of Jesus Christ to live a dedicated life in the 'secular' world of work, whatever form that takes. A rhythm of prayer could be seen, in the context of busy lives, as another thing

---

[68] this is the noun variant of *avad.*

[69] Thomas Merton, *Contemplation in a World of Action* (New York: Doubleday, 1971) p.27

[70] de Waal, *Seeking God*, p.153

to do, in addition to the other tasks. To respond to the call to this way of life is to understand that prayer is to shape us for the other tasks we do.

This is not to shy away from the necessity to engage in prayer practices by justifying that every action is done in an attitude of prayer but rather it is to suggest that the need for prayer is to direct our lives towards God. To put it another way, if we are not directed towards God we a directed towards something/someone else. We are made for worship, in everything that we do. Prayer roots us in the presence of God and from there all actions we take can be called prayer.

What form should prayer take?

In the light of what we've explored so far the answer is "it doesn't matter." What religious communities have discovered is that there must be times of structured prayer and times for more free prayer. The purpose of structured prayer is to establish and maintain a rhythm around which a community can gather. Esther de Waal warns us,

> Prayer might develop into some individualistic self-indulgence unless anchored in the local community to which I belong.[71]

A liturgical format holds a community together around shared prayers. They act, as the psalms have done for millennia, to encourage us to encounter the reality of life in all its facets. Set prayers force us to stay in uncomfortable places spiritually; they deny us the possibility to ignore certain aspects of our life or to turn to false illusions of grandeur or loathing. Like the psalms, these established, communal prayers enable a community to embrace the rhythm of reality.

[71] Ibid., p.150

> Much Christian piety and spirituality is romantic and unreal in its positiveness. As children of the Enlightenment, we have censored and selected around the voice of darkness and disorientation, seeking to go from victory to victory. But such a way not only ignores the Psalms; it is a lie in terms of our experience.[72]

To do this unmasking, this spiritual stripping and destruction of idols in the company of others, is a powerful experience. Instead of the embarrassment, which we fear, corporately engaging in the vulnerability required to pray makes one feel encouraged. The sharing of these prayers with other human beings in the tangible, visible and audible certainty of communal life not only rejects the inner conviction that it ever took place but also invites us to journey with our fellow pilgrims into a landscape we daren't go alone.

I went through a period of extreme doubt a few years ago, when prayer seemed to be a pointless exercise. My wife was struggling with her health and it felt like she was losing her battle against illness. As I faithfully turned up for prayer in the morning, noon and night my desperate pleas for healing and help were making no difference to my wife's ongoing situation. Why bother continuing to articulate my appeal? I tried re-phrasing it; I tried deeper confession in the vain hope that God may consider me worthy to grant my request. All was in vain.

I sat, sometimes alone, sometimes with another, and fell silent. I turned up out of duty. Whilst I was there, I churned out prayers written by other people for other occasions. I read the psalms for the day and in these psalms I found a new voice. I heard another person vocalize the deep yearnings of my heart. In those moments I no longer felt alone, instead I sat with God's people in familiar territory and was able to stand firm in the faith that God will come.

---

[72] Walter Brueggemann, *The Message of the Psalms* (Minneapolis: Augsburg Publishing, 1984) p.11

> The Psalter is the prayer of Christ for his Church in which he stands in for us and prays in our behalf ... In the Psalter we learn to pray on the basis of Christ's own prayer [and] as such is the great school of prayer.[73]

Later, in the depths of bereavement, after my wife's death, this experience of being held in a rhythm, saved my life. When everything in my life was uncertain and the turmoil of the storm was overwhelming; the established stability of liturgical prayers held me like a boat. It is at these times of doubt, dryness in our devotion that an established rhythm of prayer holds and sustains us. Without this stability, life becomes chaotic. This is the lesson being learnt anew by New Monastics. It is a lesson that has been taught by quiet example by the religious communities throughout the centuries; the lesson to intentionally seek God in every aspect of our life so that every aspect can be transformed by His love. We are called to dedicate our lives and every moment to Him in order that we might be embraced by His grace.

All this of course would be impossible if the initiative and the activity lay with us. Mercifully that is not the case. While we are seeking God he is also seeking us. This asks of us not so much that we actually say prayers as that we live open to grace... St. Benedict is giving us the chance to stand where, if we are truly seeking God, we know that we shall be found by him.[74] For our time, what does the Catholic, the universal Church, the universal faith look like in our different contexts? I hope these pages may help to tell our shared story again, with an a-contextual background, to draw us together to see, afresh, the power of the gospel for all of creation.

---

[73] Dietrich Bonhoeffer, *The Psalms: The Prayer Book of the Bible* (Minneapolis: Augsburg Fortress, 1970) p. 55

[74] de Waal, *Seeking God*, p.153-4

WATER

Redemption

The Kingdom of God is like a woman who goes on a long journey...

Before the reliable Sat Nav entered our lives we had to make do with large maps and road signs and, if we were lucky enough to experience some uniformed organisation in our youth, some basic orienteering. Journeys back then were exciting adventures which took both planning and forethought as well as creative ingenuity. It wouldn't do to keep stopping the car and make a decision every step of the way; no, a general direction and some key waymarkers along the way would suffice. Only if it got too unfamiliar or unpredictable did you stop the car and revert to the map. For particularly long journeys you would find the help of a map reader invaluable, if not a little frustrating.

Before even packing the first item of clothing one would need to know where they wanted to go, even if that was some vague direction. The reason for leaving one place to travel to another are many and varied but something will either internally pull you or push you; a desire to be in better weather, to be anywhere but where you are... And so you make a decision,

"I want to go..." What followed was the digging out of the nearest map and finding your departure point. Keeping your finger on that point you'd search, sometimes turning pages, for the destination or at least a particular marker on the journey. From this you could follow the lines which indicated the roads and at any deviation from the first road a mental bookmark as to how you'll know when to turn onto the new branch of the journey.

For some there was a need for an itinerary with detailed step by step instructions with distances between different points, road names and landmarks all clearly marked for ease of navigation. These were placed with the map into the car. If there was to be a designated map reader, they were given clear instructions to follow the itinerary precisely for if the journey went awry the blame would be firmly on the map reader and never the itinerary!

For others there was a more *laissez faire* approach. An innate reliance on the road signs that undoubtedly would clearly guide them to their destination. All that was needed was a rough idea as to the order in which certain major places would come on their journey. The timing of the journey was left to chance and guesstimates and that was part of the adventure.

"We will not be tied down. We are free. We are in charge of our destiny!" The journey became part of the fun rather than just a means to get to a destination; the thrill of discovery and surprise spurring the travelers on to explore new places and if they got lost… so be it. We'll survive.

So the woman, neither being totally comfortable with the great unknown nor wanting to be predictable, decides to make rough notes on key parts of the journey but tells herself that if all goes wrong she'll work it out as she goes along.

"It is irresponsible not to consider the potential dangers and pitfalls in a long journey. What if I were to get lost with no one around to ask for help? Or, what's worse, what if I end up in a scary backwater pub face to face with an unhinged man who could easily take advantage of me in my vulnerable state? No, I must make some provision and have some course to follow." With this she rifles through her map that seems out of date, but roads don't change that much do they?

She decides to stick to main roads which are well lit and well used by other travelers, so if she gets totally lost she can wave down a fellow pilgrim and ask for directions or find a nearby town or built up area. There she could easily find a trustworthy citizen who had no need of abusing a helpless woman. She makes a note of the roads and trusts she'll remember to keep her eyes out for turnings which will, inevitably, be well marked with plenty of warning as they approach.

Happy with her general course of action, prepared and yet open to improvisation, she begins to pack her bags for the journey. She contacts the destination with a rough arrival time and jokingly says to them,

"If I haven't arrived by then, call the police!"

As the departure time approaches, she prepares the house for shut down mode, preventing any disaster befalling the house in her absence and informing the trusted neighbours that she will be away for a week or so. She begins to dream about the life of adventure she was going to have, safe in the knowledge that there are clear parameters to defend against anything too scary.

She loads up the car and places the map within reach next to her along with the list of road names clearly displayed on top; yes, she can look down at any moment and check the rough guide towards her destination. She puts some suitable travelling music on to keep her alert and to comfort her loneliness of the journey which she feels in total silence and starts the journey.

Whilst the landscape around remains familiar and the roads she is led down well-worn with her wheels, she allows her mind to wander. She plans what she will do on arrival, she comforts herself that she has done everything necessary to put a metaphorical pause on her normal life and tries desperately to resist contemplating her return. She doesn't need the list of roads sat next to her; she knows where she is, and she knows where she's going.

As she reaches the outer limits of her hometown, she notices helpful prompts in signs directing her to known places along her route and she obediently follows them. This is easier than she thought. She is not as accustomed to travelling these roads, but the signs are quite clear and she can relax safe in the knowledge that beside her is the plans and the map. If she gets lost, they will help.

Soon she finds herself in new territory with new sights. As she follows the signs clearly marked along the way, she allows herself to enjoy the novelties of this strange land and even imagines herself closer to them. There are landmarks she has only ever heard of from others. She decides that these treasures would make great stories for those who would listen to her tales of adventure and she follows the signs to these monuments for memories… careful, of course, to remember where she departed from her route.

"Look at me," she thinks to herself, "being spontaneous." She revels in her free-spirited decision to experience new things, to become more rounded and 'travelled'. As she stops to enjoy some refreshment, she makes mental notes as to what she is experiencing and soon it is time to move on; she's got all she came for.

On the road again she journeys back to the detour point… or at least she thinks she does.

"I'm sure I've driven this road before. Yes. Yes, I have." She assures herself that she needn't worry but as the roads get narrower and the signs get fewer she decides to pull into a lay-by just to check the map. The list is of no use here as she went rogue from that at the detour. She finds her 'cenotaph to impulse' clearly on the map and searches all over for some semblance of familiar road name but to no avail.

She flicks back to her starting place, home, and follows the journey she had taken checking the route she undoubtedly followed but can't work out how she had managed to get to where she is now. In a panic she jumps back into the car and decides that instinct got her here, instinct will lead her back.

She drives waiting for something either familiar or safe to appear in her surroundings. As she waits, she no longer feels comforted by the music that plays and even the happiest rhythms have taken on a sinister tone. She begins to feel regret at making the detour, of even making the journey itself. She begins to play through her obituary, which will inevitably be all over the newspapers the following day.

She encourages herself by reminding her of the inspirational time she had had visiting a new place. She enjoys again the thrill of being free from expectation and demands. The taste of freedom, again on her lips, she drives on as the sky becomes dark and the landscape closes in on her. She is in charge, lost, but in control.

She happens to drive into a small market town with lit streets and amenities. Her fuel is running low and so she keeps her eyes open for a petrol station. Now is the time to ask for help but not just anyone; someone trustworthy who knows their way around. She pulls into a hotel and walks up to the reception.

"Good evening." she says with forced joy and energy.

"Good evening, miss. Would you like a room?"

"No. Thank you. I'm lost. I need directions." She places her map onto the desk and looks pleadingly at the man. He turns the map round and flicks through a few pages. He searches the map and places his finger decidedly on a town.

"We are here." he says smiling. "Where do you want to go?"

She tells him half expecting him to frown unknowingly. Instead he gives a curious sideward smile.

"How did you get here?"

"I took a detour."

"I should say!" She then regales him with the whole story of her flight of fancy and how she had thought that her instinct would guide her back in the right direction.

"The bad news is," begins the receptionist, "you've been heading in the wrong direction for miles. You're going to need to turn around and head back on yourself. Look." The receptionist begins to turn some more pages and, again, places a finger onto the map. "This is where you're headed. All you need to do is…" He begins the directions back to a main road but then stops abruptly. "Do you know what? I'm finishing for the night anyway and I am heading in that direction. Why not follow me and I'll lead you to the right road."

"Would you mind?"

"No problem." He starts locking up and preparing to leave. When he is ready, out of curiosity more than anything else, he turns to the woman and asks,

"Did you not think about working the route out yourself?"

"I did at home, but I got cocky."

"No. I mean after you got lost. If you were able to find this landmark you had been at on the map, why did you not just start again? Recalibrate and begin again?"

The woman smiled.

"When you're lost it's hard to think straight or to find your bearings."

Like children we want to be independent from our Father; we want to make it on our own. This sensation is not always as violent or antagonistic as we imagine, for we have been told that independence is the aim of every generation; parent and child. We, as children, are to cut free of the apron strings, take off the stabilizers and go it alone. Maturity is marked by how little we rely on parents and can be self-sufficient. Dependency is weakness and is to be avoided. We are to move from heteronomy (a law that comes from an external source) to autonomy (a law that comes from one's self). Our adolescence is experienced as the transition between these two states and we swing from one extreme to the other. But is autonomy really the goal?

Parents, although they are happy to be emergency contacts and step into to help children, at some point want independence too. They want to be free of the constant concern as to where their little ones are and what they are doing. They want to remember what it was like to live life without the eternal alertness to potential dangers for another. They let their offspring explore the world and hope they have done enough.

If we're going to get into the driving seat and prove we're grown up, we're going to need to have a clear plan. The parents will not trust you to be left alone if you cannot show that you have the capabilities to look after yourself; to recognise and assess risk and work round it.

From a young age we're asked, "What are you going to be when you grow up?" Earlier and earlier in our lives we make decisions which shape our future. A plan makes us feel safe and helps us navigate the choices, which line the road of our lives. Life is a long journey and it would be irresponsible to not be aware of the many dangers and pitfalls that will come our way. Avoidance is the best tactic for these, and preparation and diversions should be made to steer clear of such snares.

From Eden, where we left them, the first children of God were sent out on their own. Like all relationship breakdowns this driving out of Adam and Eve was painful for both sides. Adam and Eve made a choice to be independent from Him and He had to respect that decision; how He must have longed for it not to be so but, out of love for them, He packed their bags with them.

There's a beautiful moment before He finally waved goodbye to His children as they left the family home.

> And the Lord God made garments of skins for the man and for his wife, and clothed them. (Gen 3:21)

The Father still cared for His children and the 'divorce' was not entered into lightly. This was about giving to His children what they requested: autonomy, but the Father held out hope that they might turn back and choose to be with Him. They had, however, tasted 'freedom' and how bad could it get? There's, surely, only two options: heteronomy or autonomy, right?

His children had children and they had children and with each passing generation they drifted further from that invitation to life with and through Him. They journeyed further and further away, hiding deeper and deeper into the unknown in the vain hope of losing sight of the guilt of their forebears. Yet He was still involved in their lives. He remained on the periphery waiting to step in whenever He was asked but all the time it was on their terms. He wanted their love for Him to be genuine and that meant allowing them to find their own way back… or forward.

Independence is about owning consequences for your actions. Being 'grown up' is about learning how to respond to mistakes. In the early days of maturity there is the danger that in trying to fix a problem we can make it worse.

I once lived with a couple in a lovely house. They had an expensive chopping board which, by its design, looked like a baking tray. One night I returned home from work late and hungry, so I decided to get a Chicken Kiev out of the freezer. I placed it on a baking tray from the cupboard (you know where this is heading!) I popped the Kiev and the baking tray into the oven and set a timer. I went off and entertained myself until the Kiev was cooked.

As the timer rung out, I returned to the kitchen and looked into the oven to check that the Kiev looked cooked. There it was, bubbling away, but where was the baking tray? Then I looked down and saw it too was bubbling away. The baking tray (which was really a plastic chopping board) had melted through the grates.

Panicking, I turned off the oven and opened it. I carefully removed the Kiev with a fish slice and threw it away. I stood staring as the black globules dripped to the bottom of the oven. My first instinct was to scrape the black glue from the bottom and so set to it with the same fish slice. The problem was, whilst the plastic was hot it was like liquid and hard to lift off the bottom it needed to be cold to make it a solid and, therefore, removable. So I waited for it to cool.

As it cooled, however, it bonded itself to the metal of the oven. I discovered I needed the plastic to be lukewarm; not cold enough that it was neither unmovable nor too hot that it dripped around the fish slice like water. This meant, in order to remove all traces of melted plastic from my host's oven I needed to keep turning the oven on, warming up the plastic so it was malleable and then turning it off so it didn't liquify too much.

This worked until I realised, not only that the fish slice had molded plastic now attached to it which needed heating up to be removed, but as soon as I removed the plastic from the bottom of the oven the remaining plastic from the grate continued to drip from above. I needed to attack the grates first before I could remove the stuff from the bottom! I quickly removed the two grates, which were now held, suspended together like a beautiful mixed media art piece.

As I pulled the grates out, the same issue occurred it needed to be cool enough for me to get some purchase on the plastic but warm enough that it was malleable to remove it from the metal. With the grates out of the oven, where I could change the temperature, how was I planning on doing this? I decided to keep placing the grates in the oven, thus warming them up, and removing them and quickly prising off the plastic. I did not take into account, however, that hot metal on wooden side boards was not helpful nor that the plastic could possibly drip onto the oiled oak floorboards. These then needed to be cleaned and quickly for the plastic would cool onto them and I'd need to chip away at the black mess.

I did finally manage to clean the oven up and replaced the expensive chopping board that had caused all the mess. The point is, that at each step of the cleanup, it got messier. As the pressure to make amends grew, the more frantic I became to stop the situation from escalating. I was working it out as I went along, which was fine, but I'd have preferred some experienced person to guide me and encourage me that it was redeemable.

Like the woman on a long journey, once you know you're lost it's hard to keep your bearings. The world spins and the right way to go becomes lost in the blur of panic. It's made worse when you have set yourself up as sole authority. In our pride we've dismissed help in favour of making our own way. We hold onto the idea that we can wash off all the marks of mistakes and start again but no matter how hard we try we can't get rid of them. Sometimes we are too far in and it's too shameful to ask for help.

"No one can help me now!"

As the children of God travelled further and further away and detours led to detours, God kept up with them. When they got lost, He stood at the side of the road with them and asked,

"Do you want my help?"

"No. We can do it. Leave us alone. We're grown up. We'll work it out."

Soon He stopped offering the help or rather they stopped even hearing His quiet invitation. As they developed a habit of ignoring His help, they began to tell each other He wasn't even there and didn't care for them.

"It would be helpful if He came and helped to clean up this mess we're in. Maybe He wants us to go and find him." So, like the woman, they got the map out and tried to work out where they went wrong, where they may have left Him, but they couldn't figure out how it all got to be like this. What was obvious was He wasn't around anymore and if He was, He'd probably only say,

"I told you so." He wanted them to be independent, didn't He? They got themselves into it, they needed to get themselves out; by any means.

It is easy to read the clear instructions God gives as an enforced law from above eradicating any need for self-will. The Bible becomes a route which we must all stick to; no deviations. If we deviate, then that's our problem. God is the un-shifting master planner and that is how He wants us to live. Joseph Myers in his excellent book, 'Organic Community', suggests;

> A theology of God as master planner implies that God has a purpose – even one purpose – for your life and it's your lifelong job to pursue it, identify it, and live it out. The gospel becomes, "God has a plan for your life." God has planned the job, the life partner, the house, the child, and

> so on. He wants nothing more than our cooperation with his plan.[75]

The truth is more generous than that. It is not heteronomy or autonomy that is required but a third option. This third option is a freely chosen collaboration between two free active agents. It is marked by a humble recognition of our own power and choice and using it to grow and change. The reason we choose to ignore this authoritative help is because we refuse to humble ourselves and name the reality we are in or we dismiss doing it for we are to be free from such 'oppressive tyranny'. Our help is far away and won't come and find us; we'd ask if only we could find Him. We either don't want to hand over the driving seat or we don't acknowledge that is even an option. Brian C. Taylor articulates this choice well,

> In that exposure of self we have a choice: we can hide and pretend we are not exposed, like the emperor with his "new clothes", or we can deny our egotistical self and turn toward God, change, and life.[76]

As the kind receptionist reminds the lost woman, "Recalibrate and start again." We are so keen to cover our mistake or rectify the wrong we've done that we back-track and fix from the start. We have an inbuilt desire for justice and justice, in our mind, is about putting right what went wrong. Going back and making good. We humans return again and again to the karmic view of how the world works. We fixate on the cause and effect of the natural order and we say for every bad choice, we must make an equal and opposite good choice. We will not be judged as a failure if we can just make the moral scales balance out. So, if we can keep track of the

---

[75] Joseph Myers, *Organic Community: creating a place where people naturally connect* (Michigan: Baker Books, 2008) p

[76] Taylor, *Spirituality for Everyday Life,* p.23

mistakes we've made, then we might be able to find a way of covering them up in the hope that someone won't notice them in balance, instead of washing them clean.

One of the issues with karma is that the onus remains on us. We don't have to turn back and admit that we don't know how to live. We'll be fine as long as we can keep out of debt; it would be better if we could even go into credit with this almighty judge. When we do fall into moral debt, despite the feeling of failure, karma keeps us in a place of self-sufficiency and the panic continues to drive us further into the ever-enveloping landscape of lostness. In this spiraling reality we comfort ourselves with joys and successes, achievements we made and assure ourselves that we can rise again to such greatness ignoring the help that remains on the fringes of our lives waiting to step in and change us.

We, like children, are discovered so often with chocolate smeared on our face, we feel the guilt and shame of mistake and we have a choice of allowing our faces to be washed or we pretend the guilty stain is not there or that it is something else or someone else's fault.

How do we recalibrate?

To calibrate, is to mold something, usually a metal. Bullets are measured in calibers referring to the size of the mold. To recalibrate, then, means to re-mold something. As I did to the plastic chopping board in the oven so God can do to our lives. Rowan Williams, using C.S. Lewis' imagery in 'The Voyage of the Dawn Treader' of Eustace being changed into a dragon and needing Aslan to scratch off his scales to change him back to his right state, points out,

> …the only decision to be a stranger to heaven is ours. Once such a decision is made and once it becomes a habit of mind, the persistent work of God to break through is bound to be experienced as an assault on the citadel of the soul rather than a campaign to liberate that soul from its

> self-imposed captivity. God cannot but start from the situation as it is.[77]

It took the children of God a long time, but they did realise that God wanted to help. He wanted His children back, to give them a wash and start again. They came, tails between their legs, heads bowed low begging for forgiveness as if their contrition needed to equate to the imagined pain they had caused. The truth was the pain was far worse than they could ever express and nothing they could do or say could match it.

The good news, however, was that the balancing of the books never happened.

Although it felt like the children of God needed to make the long journey back to where it all went wrong, the Father was coming out to meet them. He had travelled the distance; He had followed them into their mess out of love and concern for them. He watched as they made mistake after mistake. Through it all He hoped they would see Him and invite Him in and with each new decision to go it alone His hopes were dashed, and He was crushed again. *We* decided that the rules of justice were karmic rather than grace. *We* decided that God should judge us according to our laws when, in reality, at His heart His judgments are always grace-centric.

For the children, however much they felt remorse and desired to change, old habits die-hard and the world was now programmed around that choice to live in karma and not grace. The journey had been so long they had forgotten where they started and even where they were heading. The stains of guilt became habit and custom and they no longer saw the need to wash them off. Every time they became aware of their lostness they realised they knew no markers to help them navigate their way out. They travelled around

[77] Rowan Williams, *The Lion's World: a journey into the heart of Narnia* (London: SPCK, 2012) p. 87-88

aimlessly. God put up signposts to direct them back; sometimes they followed, other times they missed it.

What the children of God needed was a clear voice saying,

"The bad news is you've been heading in the wrong direction. You know where you've come from, you've forgotten how you got lost so now focus on the destination and use this point as a new start and head towards the target. Turn around and head in that direction and, just in case you get lost again why not follow me and I'll lead you to the right road."

That's the plan God made. They no longer recognised Him nor heard Him when He spoke so He sent a representative; His Son.

The revelation of Jesus as 'the image of the invisible God' (Col 1:15) is another central principle of Christian theology. In Jesus we see the Father, we hear the Father, we know the Father; for the Son and the Father are one and the same. In Jesus we meet the Father who neither ignored nor rejected us but called out to us to give up this life of independence and autonomy and come back home.

Like the receptionist, Jesus meets us when we open ourselves to help. He gives the clear instructions to stop trying to fix the problem on our own terms but to turn around, recalibrate, repent. He dusts us off, cleans us up, resets us and, knowing that we are so programmed to get lost, He walks the journey with us. He becomes our guide.

The children of God meet this stranger on the road who seemed to demand attention. He knew where they had come from and He knew where they should be headed. He lived, not under this karmic view of justice but with grace. He gave clear instructions as to how they could reach their destination and was willing to walk it with them. He was not controlling but worked with free choices, gently persuading them to follow Him and be changed. His forgiveness finally washed away the stains of guilt and shame.

Joseph Myers, who challenged the view of God as master planner offers the alternative way God directs us,

> A theology of God as organic order, however, allows for collaboration with him. We are privileged to participate with him in the forming of our future. He invites our ideas, our energy, our creativity, our perspective. He gives up a measure of control to facilitate relationship with us and to demonstrate his love.[78]

In 'God's Theatre', T.J. Gorringe argues that we fall into the trap of either saying human free will is always working contrary to God's will and therefore we should cast it aside and be automatons or God works all things to good and so we can do what we like because God is going to fix everything anyway. How do we balance God's omnipotence and Scripture's clear proclamation of God's plan for humankind and our innate free will? Gorringe and a theologian called Greg Boyd suggest an understanding of God's work amongst human beings that picks up on Myers call for organic order that sees God as someone who wants collaboration rather than cooperation.

Peter Brook, a theatre director and writer of 'The Empty Space', tells the story of one of his early productions: Love's Labour's Lost for the RSC. He describes how he would have a scene mapped out before rehearsals; he knew where people should move and how and what every moment would look like. He would use cardboard figurines to move them about the stage at different moments and would have it all charted out. He, like many directors before and after him, discovered,

> As the actors began to move I knew it was no good. These were not remotely like the cardboard figures, these large human beings thrusting themselves forward, some too fast with lively steps I had not foreseen…We had only done the first stage movement, letter A on my chart, but already everyone was wrongly placed and movement B could not

[78] Myers, *Organic Community*, p.130-131

> follow… Was I to start again, drilling these actors so that they conformed to my notes? One inner voice prompted me to do so, but another pointed out that my pattern was much less interesting than this new pattern that was unfolding in front of me…I stopped, and walked away from my book, in amongst the actors, and I have never looked at a written plan since.[79]

We have seen, however, the need for God to be steadfast and stable. We must be able to know that God will remain the same if we are to trust Him. If we are going to trust Him with our lives, we need to be confident He knows what He is doing and isn't going to make it up as He goes along (we could do that for ourselves!)

The problem with seeing God as the master planner, setting a route we must follow to the letter, however, becomes tricky when faced with the accounts of how He interacts with His children through the Bible. Consider Abraham at Sodom and Gomorrah (Gen 18:22-33) or Moses in the wilderness (Ex 32:9-14). God seems to be able to change His mind. How are we to have a relationship with Him if He is an autocrat? If God's will and plan isn't going to change, why do we bother praying? If God is a master planner then isn't prayer just us tapping a busy God on the shoulder saying,

"If you can find it in your heart to change the whole world order so I can have a parking space, that would be nice… but only if it's in your plan…" What kind of relationship is that? An authority figure demanding you do exactly as you're told can't surely be loving, can it? (Even if the plans are to prosper me and not to harm me!)

A far more significant issue arises when seeing God as a master planner when you're faced with the crucified God.

[79] Peter Brook, *The Empty Space* (London: Penguin Books, 1990) p.120

The gospel has become heavily cross-centred due, in the most part, to the reformation's need to counteract the abuse of indulgences, a system by which people literally paid for their sins. As the poor began to feel the weight of the burden of unpaid moral debts, the reformers were eager to point out the truth of God's final destruction of this karmic view of justice.

"Good news! That debt has been paid."

Penal substitution became, almost to the eradication of other views, the doctrine of atonement and salvation. The issue with penal substitution as the only view of Jesus' work on the cross, is it relies on a God who lives under this karmic law about debt and debtors. What of a God who starts at grace?

Some of the children of God saw Jesus and recognised the Father. Many, however, did not.

"Who is this arrogant man? Who does He think He is? He thinks He has the right to tell us what to do? He wants to have dominion over us and assert His own authority. He even believes He can wash away sin." Jesus challenged their power and the foundations of their worldview. He was a rebel, a terrorist. He upset the order of the world that had been built up over generations. He refused to see or accept the story told by humanity and spoke out its brokenness, proclaiming it a distortion. Jesus established a new world order. He was seemingly changing the way we see and understand the universe and ourselves, but the reality was it wasn't an invention it was a restoration, a cleansing. In His actions and in His words, He seemed to live in a different world; people, quite rightly, thought He was deranged and unhinged. He had to be stopped or chaos would ensue, and the safety and security of life would be lost to anarchy or worse, tyranny. Balance needed to be restored… or rather the perceived balance.

Jesus was tried as an extremist and was publicly executed to show everyone that His self-identifying as God, Creator of the Universe, the Father who called all things into being, was blasphemous and deluded. Jesus knew this would happen and had the blind audacity to predict He would rise again after three days. To prove He could do it He brought three people back from the dead and then repeated His prophecy.

What makes God a divine ruler as opposed to all false gods and idols, Karl Barth writes, is,

> …the very fact that his rule is determined and limited: self-determined and self-limited, but determined and limited none the less.[80]

Gorringe concludes,

> Knowledge of this self-limitation derives from the cross, for if everything were rigorously determined what could the cross be but a piece of spectacular, though indecent, theatre? On the contrary the 'necessity' of the cross, frequently spoken about by New Testament authors, is God's refusal to overrule human history. If the cross is our guide, God is no determinist.[81]

What is seen on the cross, and in the resurrection, is God's power working through human free will. God didn't pretend to die on the cross. He didn't hold onto control or power in that situation, forcing His will to override our human choices. Rather, He became weak and died in order that we could know that, in the resurrection, Jesus was who He had said He was: God.

If Jesus was God then it was God who was tortured. It was God who was abused and shamed. It was God who died on the cross; God, who hung the stars now hung, naked, ashamed for everyone to see. Humanity had finally killed their Father and were

---

80 Karl Barth, *Church Dogmatics II/2* (London: T&T Clark, 2009) p.50

81 T.J. Gorringe, *God's Theatre: A Theology of Providence* (London: SCM Press, 1991) p.12

free to run the world how they saw fit. The amazing thing about that is: God let them!

> God chooses to work through billions of years of evolution or through human free will because he refuses to manipulate or control but rather wishes to woo creation to conformity with his son, as Hosea suggests.[82]

Through His Son, God revealed Himself afresh to His children. He called to them again, like He did in the beginning. He allowed humanity to choose and with every disappointment and missed opportunity, He continued to woo them with His love. He even allowed them to kill Him, the ultimate power grab, and yet… He came back for more.

We would all like to see our lives running along a determined route for this makes us passive to the fatalistic powers outside of our control. It also means when mistakes are made, or we get lost, we can legitimately ignore the problem and blame Destiny. Destiny leads us to conceive of every path we take as 'happening for a reason' for we're being driven to our destination. This belief seems to place us in the passenger seat, but we do not hand over control so easily.

We love the idea of being passive, but we are more in control of our lives than we like to give ourselves credit for. We make the decisions to go off piste and detour. We are the ones to blame for getting lost and as in any journey we need to decide what we're going to do about it. We can carry on trusting Luck or Fate or Instinct to find a way out or we can ask for help.

Yes, God has a plan. Yes, God desires for you to travel on the right path.

---

[82] ibid., p.77

> For surely I know the plans I have for you, says the Lord, plans for your welfare and not for harm, to give you a future with hope. (Jer 29:11)

Firstly this famous passage is not about the individual; it is about a nation. This statement of intention is for the macroscopic. We twist the sentiment when we use it on the microscopic. Secondly, in this passage the word for 'plans' is better translated as 'thoughts'.

"For surely I know the *thoughts* I am having for you."

"I know my dreams for you. I know how I thought you would be, and I know that one day you'll see it through my eyes."

When God meets us on the road He cares not about where we've been, what we've done. In His grace, He lifts us out of our world of transaction, karma and Fate, washes us and places us back in the garden of His delight. He can, if we allow Him, birth us anew through the water of baptism. He begins, from the moment we see the Father in His Son, Jesus, shaping the dirt and mud of our lives into new life. He recalibrates our journeys.

He redeems our lives by going back over stuff, washing it and healing it; making sure the pain and guilt of our past will no longer infect or spread into our future. This does not mean, in anyway, that He made that stuff happen so we can learn. We do great harm on ourselves and others when we explain suffering as being from God. God can make good out of evil, but it never follows that evil is necessary for God to grow us.

Following the guide means being obedient to the directions given out of love. As humans we respond to this as a giving up of our freedom; we are no longer in the driving seat, but the reality is we remain in control of choices, God can't take that away, but we are choosing to stay close to Him.

> For the Christian to be perfectly free means to be perfectly obedient.[83]

Following Jesus, 'the way, the truth and the life', is not merely about a physical repetition of His actions and steps but a taking on of a character. This was always in the mind of our Creator, that His creatures would grow to be like Him by being around Him. In his redemption of us He calls us to draw close and as we do so we are converted and changed to be like Him. Rowan Williams reminds us,

> Humanity is created in God's image – created with the capacity for relationship to God in obedience: its fulfilment is in this relationship…But the image is potential only, it must be made into a 'likeness' by the exercise of goodness. Had humanity been created in perfection, it would have performed its good acts automatically.[84]

He wants us to recalibrate and to follow Him along the journey of life. He washes us and heals us of the pain, the guilt, the disappointment of our autonomy and freely made choices, which have impacted others and us. He invites us to start a new journey from where we are heading towards our terminus. This new journey must begin with a decision to change course and learn afresh the way to peace, hope and love; the destination dreamed for us by our Creator at the beginning. The third option is: theonomy.

---

[83] Hauerwas, *Community of Character*, p.131

[84] Rowan Williams, *The Wound of Knowledge* (London: Darton, Longman and Todd, 1990) p.27-28

Conversion

Every story of conversion is the story of a blessed defeat.[85]

The Rule of St. Benedict was originally written in Latin. The vows which monks were called to make, in the original, are 'de stabilitate… conversatio morum… et oboedientia' Two of these are easily translated; de stabilitate, stability and oboedentia, obedience. It is the second of these vows which has caused translators difficulties.

What St. Benedict meant by the phrase conversatio morum is, unfortunately, lost to history. There have been countless words spent trying to translate this two-word phrase and there still is no agreement on its precise meaning. I have decided to simply translate it as 'conversion' as most translations include this phrase; what changes is the object of that conversion (behaviour, morals, life, etc.) Thomas Merton famously wrote,

> It is the vow to respond totally and integrally to the word of Christ, 'Come, follow me'…It is the vow to obey the voice of God,… in order to follow the will of God in all things.[86]

Brian C. Taylor describes this commitment to conversion as 'essentially the vow to do metanoia (repenting), the turning away from self-will and turning toward God's will.'[87] This is what is meant by theonomy, the use of our autonomy to submit to the Law of the God who does not need to force His will. Taylor likens it to the repentance which is at the heart of the sacrament of baptism.

---

[85] C.S. Lewis, Joy Davidson, *Smoke on the Mountain: an interpretation of the Ten Commandments* (Philadelphia: The Westminster Press, 1954) p.7

[86] Thomas Merton, "Conversation Morum", *Cistercian Studies* (1966) p. 133

[87] Taylor, *Spirituality for Everyday Living*, p.21

This metanoia, however, is a daily choice (if not more frequent) to turn to God, follow Christ and to be filled with the Holy Spirit. This vow is a daily commitment to the ongoing turning away from sin and, more importantly, the turning towards God; avoiding both heteronomy and autonomy in favour of theonomy.

We are regaining an increasing awareness that conversion is not a one-time event. I know too many people who said 'the prayer' and were baptized and have since fallen away. The journey of faith starts in that first 'yes' to God's call but there are some who never take many steps beyond that. Some treat the life of faith like a club; after they have paid the lifetime membership fee, they find they no longer visit the club house, speak to other members. They keep the card in their wallet which they look at from time to time, but they do not participate in the life of the club, they do not remember the purpose of the club, but their name is on the list.

The vow to conversatio morum is a lifetime commitment to participate in a process of change. It is a choice to daily engage in change and transformation and not just in the external parts of our life but, more importantly, in our inner life. Thomas Merton, speaking on the importance of conversatio morum in the religious orders, writes,

> it can be interpreted as a commitment to total inner transformation of one sort or another – a commitment to become a totally new man.[88]

I have chosen to use the Benedictine vows to shape this book in the most part because it is the Benedictine form of monasticism that has informed me most. I do, however, have many New Monastic friends who consider themselves more Franciscan in their approach to the devoted life. The two forms of religious vows from each tradition do overlie one another; stability shares a lot with

---

[88] Thomas Merton, *The Asian Journal of Thomas Merton* (New York: New Directions, 1975) p.337

chastity and obedience is obedience in both traditions but what of conversatio morum and poverty?

> All of us, if we really want to know the meaning of conversion and of faith and confidence in another, must become poor, or at least make the cause of the poor our own inner motivation. That is when one begins to experience faith and conversion: when one has the heart of the poor, when one knows that financial capital, political influence, and power are worthless, and that without God we are nothing.[89]

Here, in this quote from Oscar Romero, there is a call to place ourselves back in a perpetual Ash Wednesday. We are dust, nothing, but the life of discipleship is to remain rooted there whilst also accepting the conversion, by God's grace, into the life of Christ. In this framework the call to stability is rooted in the faithfulness of God the Father who raises us from the dust to shape and form us. The call to conversion is the identification with Christ who Himself willingly chose to enter the life of the poor and be identified with them.

In the previous chapter we explored God's rejection of the exertion of power over our wills but, instead, choosing the way of the cross. It was the free choice of God to release His power to control us in favour of living the life amongst the powerless and wooing them into new life. The transformation from the old life to the new life is not achieved by an act of strength or force but the submission of our self-wills to God's grace-centric will.

[89] Romero, *The Violence of Love*, p. 121

> The criterion of genuine conversion was love for the poor, who represented Christ, and this love obtained forgiveness and grace from God.[90]

Christ is seen, for Romero, amongst the poor. It was Christ who considered equality with God not something to be exploited but emptied Himself (Phil 2:6-7). Christ became poor so that we could be rich by God's grace (2 Cor 8:9). In this way Christ lived a purely theonomous life. If we are called to continual conversion into the likeness of Christ, then we should follow Him into His life of kenosis and empty ourselves so that others may become rich by God's grace. Our conversion is an emptying of that which we possess and that which possesses us.

All change however involves loss; a loss of what was, a loss of bearings as we enter new territory and a loss of control as to the direction we travel. All loss involves grief and pain. David Adam writes powerfully about the 'ebb and flow of the whole of creation'.

> We are a very small and frail craft in a mighty ocean. Yet we may be privileged to discover, in the ebb and flow, that nothing is lost, only changed. As the tide ebbs on one shore it flows on another… The end of one thing always heralds the beginning of something new. In the same way the beginning of something marks the end of an old order.[91]

Baptism is a celebration of new life as a person is born again as a child of God. The liturgy, however, emphasizes this 'ebb and flow' as it talks as much about the death of a person as the rebirth. In 2015 an article grabbed my attention by its curious subheading, it read: 'I'm the person I was before I became a person of faith – a

---

[90] Della Rocca, *Oscar Romero*, p.120

[91] David Adam, Border Lands: the best of David Adam's Celtic vision (Wisconsin:Sheed & Ward, 2000) p.6

baptism isn't a brainwashing.' The article did not focus much on the change that came at the conversion moment that started the writer's journey in faith; it was much more about his discovery of a place of belonging (an important thing to discuss.) Near the end of the article he wrote,

> At the end of the day, I'm a Christian because faith, and our openness to God and to one another, make us stronger and more willing to engage the world as it unfolds and changes around us.[92]

What is interesting about this sentence is the focus of change is on the world around us rather than on within us. Faith, it seems, is a tool to protect us from a world which, at times, is scary and threatening as it impacts and changes us. The narrative portrayed in this article is, in order to follow Christ in engaging in the world, we must secure our inner identity in case it is lost or changed. In this our autonomy becomes a thing to be protected and sustained. The life of poverty and of kenosis, however, demands that we follow Christ in dying to self in order that we can be raised with Him in new life. Esther de Waal suggests, 'we must expect to see our chosen idols successively broken. It means a constant letting go.'[93]

Murray Bodo sums up this posture of poverty in his book 'Juniper'.

> If I am truly poor, then I am dependent on others for everything, and I feel useless and worthless, and I realise deep within that everything is a gift from the Father. Then in this attitude of complete dependence, I become useful

[92]https://www.theguardian.com/commentisfree/2015/jun/28/gay-liberal-convert-to-christianity

[93] de Waal, *Seeking God*, p.70

> again, for then I am empty of selfishness and I am free to be God's instrument instead of my own.[94]

Our conversion is also about being brought into true communion with others, as one is converted through relationship and community. The conversion that is required is from an isolated individual personality into true personhood; the mystery at the heart of the character of our Triune God.

In his article "Human Capacity and Human Incapacity", John Zizioulas outlines the difference between traditional philosophical thought on personhood and the unique Christian understanding.

> ...Western thought arrived at the conception of the person as an individual and/or personality, i.e., a unit endowed with intellectual, psychological and moral qualities centred on the axis of consciousness.

For the Christian, however,

> ...being a person is basically different from being an individual or 'personality' in that the person cannot be conceived in itself as a static entity, but only as it relates to. Thus personhood implies the 'openness of being', and even more than that, the ek-stasis of being, i.e. a movement towards communion which leads to a transcendence of the boundaries of the 'self' and thus to freedom.[95]

Zizioulas' 'openness of being' could be seen as some dualistic escapism of the soul to the Divine. The argument, however, is fully

---

[94] Murray Bodo, *Juniper: friend of Francis, fool of God (Cincinnati:St Anthony Messenger, 1983),p.28*

[95] John Zizioulas, "Human Capacity and Human Incapacity: A Theological Exploration of Personhood", T.F. Torrance and J. K. S. Reid (eds.), *Scottish Journal Theology Vol 28* (1975), p.406

rooted in the reality of the physical community of the Body of Christ: the Church. It is in this communal environment that we are called to move towards communion with others as we transcend the boundaries of 'self'. It is this new identity, formed in community, which is so alien to our hyper-individualized sense of identity. God uses His Body, as He used the body of Christ, as a vehicle of grace to transform us. We, so steeped in individualism, often deny Christ in other human beings and refuse to receive grace through them out of fear.

Samuel Wells takes this idea of receiving gifts and discusses an improvisational device called 'overaccepting'[96] as a potential tool for Christian ethics.

> Overaccepting is accepting in the light of a larger story. The fear about accepting is that one will be determined by the gift, and thus lose one's integrity and identity. The fear of blocking is that one will seal oneself off from the world, and thus lose one's relevance and humanity. Overaccepting is an active way of receiving that enables one to retain both identity and relevance… Christians imitate the character of God to the extent that they overaccept the gifts of creation and culture in the same way God does.[97]

Within this framework we can see how we move closer to the mystery at the heart of the Trinity; that of maintaining difference whilst sharing identity with others in communion. Zizioulas' further development in his understanding of personhood challenges

---

[96] In improvisational theatre every action or speech by an actor is called an 'offer' which the other actor(s) choose to 'block' (refuse), 'accept' (allow but do not actively engage with or build upon) or 'overaccept' (allow and actively engage in, building upon it to create the ongoing story as it unfolds).

[97] Samuel Wells, "Improvisation in the Theatre as a Model for Christian Ethics", Trevor Hart and Steven Guthrie, *Faithful Performance: Enacting Christian Tradition* (Aldershot: Ashgate, 2007) p.161

individualism by suggesting we must de-individualize Christ. He writes, "In order that Christology may be relevant to anthropology, it must 'de- individualise' Christ, so that every man may be 'de-individualised' too."[98]

Christ's de-individualization is, for Zizoulas, pneumatologically conditioned because it was only 'of the Spirit' that Christ united the human, one individual, and the divine, another individual. In this way the Spirit makes it possible for one to be many and so constitutes, for Zizioulas, the Church which is 'essentially none other than that of the "One" who is simultaneously "many".'[99]In this way the New Monastic movement powerfully challenges the Church to become the Body of Christ by the Rule of Life, a forming of a common life to which all submit together. The individualizing of what is, primarily, a communal life by the almost oxymoronic concept of an individual/personal Rule betrays how much we, as humans, desire individualism over the uniting of the Body of Christ. Submission to a Rule of Life must reject this idol of autonomy and train us in theonomy expressed through the Body of Christ; a communal unity.

Zizoulas goes on to suggest that, "If the Church is constituted through… Pneumatology, all pyramidal notions disappear in ecclesiology: the "one" and the "many" co-exist as two aspect of the same being."[100] His belief that this will 'remove any pyramidal structures', as understood by our current culture, is undermined, however, by his continued assertion of the importance of the presence of a bishop, as representative of Christ, within the community. This order of precedence raises the "one" above the "many" and thus creates, for our culture, a hierarchy and division. Indeed, it is the role of bishops and, to a certain degree, clergy in general that has been seen as the undermining of the full realisation

---

[98] Zizioulas, "Human Capacity and Human Incapacity", p.438

[99] John Zizioulas, *Being as Communion: Studies in Personhood and the Church* (London: Darton Longman and Todd) p112

[100] Ibid., p.139-141

of an egalitarian or flat leadership, an expressed desire of our current culture.

Jürgen Moltmann's ecclesiology, however, offers us a helpful addition.

> The doctrine of the Trinity constitutes the church as a "community free of dominion." The Trinitarian principle replaces the principle of power by the principle of concord. Authority and obedience are replaced by dialogue, consensus, and harmony… The hierarchy which preserves and enforces unity is replaced by the brotherhood and sisterhood of the community of Christ.[101]

Moltmann's social Trinity is a communion free from dominion and offers an ecclesiology for our generation who are hungry for the intimacy of community whilst maintaining autonomy of individualism. The issue, as we will see in the next section is that authority is necessary in preserving equality in relationship but how that authority is held is key. For now, it is worth noting that Christ's handling of authority and power should instruct us in how we too should participate in community.

As we journey from the Ash Wednesday moment towards the communal Pentecost moment, we travel through a third point of reference: Christ's obedience to death on the cross necessary to open the way for us to have full communion with God. As we continually remind ourselves of our status without God, we must also submit ourselves to His will, leading us to death with Christ in order to rise to a new life in communion. It is in the point of metanoia and kenosis that the start of conversion begins. The Holy Spirit begins its work of transformation and converts us into the likeness of the de-individualized Christ and His glory and this conversion to 'glory' is not as most would imagine, an individual

---

[101] Jürgen Moltmann, *The Trinity and the Kingdom: The Doctrine of God* (Minneapolis: Fortress Press, 1993) p202

perfecting but the conversion is into the corporate Body of Christ. This conversion into 'something' at once reminds 'that without God we are nothing'.

In chapter 58 of the Rule of St Benedict, we hear the admission to the religious life not being made easy for newcomers[102]. The way of life that is being demanded by the Rule is not easy and should, like we explored in the last section, not be entered into lightly or selfishly but reverently and responsibly. There is currently a discussion between traditional monastic orders and the New Monastic communities over the nature of 'vows'. The debate revolves around whether the seasonal vows being made by New Monastic communities is in anyway comparable to the life-long vows made by the traditional orders. It is not my place to flesh out the arguments here but this dialogue is important as it is in this area that I believe New Monasticism must listen, reflect and only then can fulfill a mediation role between the religious life and the wider Church in teaching what discipleship looks like in 21st century Western culture; particularly, I think, in the area of the increasingly controversial subject of vows (baptism, marriage and ordination).

The Oxford Movement birthed the first religious communities in the Church of England, after the Reformation. It did so out of a desire to re-engage in commitment in the life of faith; the discipline commanded and seen in the Early Church. The Tractarians saw a diluting of all social vows, and particularly those made within the life of the Church. We have already explored how the religious life challenges the dissolving of marital vows and now we turn to how it can encourage a re-engagement in the baptismal vows of all Christians.

As an Anglican priest I have the joy of welcoming many families each year to church as they seek to get their child 'christened'/'done'. It is always a pleasure to meet with them and

[102] RB 58:1

have an opportunity to talk to them about God and explore the life of faith. I am not naïve, however, to think that at the forefront of most of these parents' minds is anything theological but rather a maintaining of tradition out of a sense of cultural duty. This is not to say that they are not open to God but, unfortunately, it is increasingly common for the parents to have no language or even concept of God and so the conversation as to why they want their child 'done' is rarely articulated in any informed way.

It is in our increasingly secular society that we, the Church, have an opportunity to re-examine our baptismal theology. We no longer have the Christendom paradigm with its pressure to baptize anything that moves but now we can return to an approach outlined in the Didache and other Early Church liturgies.

Dietrich Bonhoeffer, in his 'Letters and Papers from Prison', begins to outline a book he never had the chance to complete. In this unrealized book, I believe, he intended to formulate a 'religionless Christianity'[103] which would be based on his extensive thought on monastic practices. His exploration of monasticism is most profoundly seen in his book 'The Cost of Discipleship'. In a chapter on 'costly grace' he criticizes, in my mind, amongst other things, the Christendom approach to baptism and uses the monastic understanding of faith as a counter model.

> The expansion of Christianity and the increasing secularization of the church caused the awareness of costly grace to be gradually lost. The world was Christianized; grace became common property of a Christian world. It could be had cheaply. But the Roman church did keep a remnant of that original awareness… Here on the boundary of the church, was the place where the awareness that grace is costly and that grace includes discipleship was preserved. People left everything they had for the sake of Christ and tried to follow Jesus' strict

[103] Bonhoeffer, *Letters and Papers from Prison*, p.280

> commandments through daily exercise. Monastic life thus became a living protest against the secularization of Christianity, against the cheapening of grace.[104]

This whole section from the chapter on 'Costly Grace' jumps from the page and into our time. He attacks the division of the Church into 'a highest and lowest achievement of Christian obedience'. The work of the monks was used to justify the lack of discipleship of the many in churches.

> But the decisive mistake of monasticism was not that it followed the grace-laden path of strict discipleship… Rather, the mistake was that monasticism essentially distanced itself from what is Christian by permitting its way to become the extraordinary achievements of a few, thereby claiming a special meritoriousness for itself.[105]

Prior to his publication of 'The Cost of Discipleship' Bonhoeffer wrote to his brother and famously proclaimed,

> The restoration of the Church will surely come from a kind of new monasticism, which has in common with the old kind only the uncompromising nature of life according to the Sermon on the Mount, following Christ.[106]

If you put these two writings together you can see Bonhoeffer beginning to formulate an ecclesiology which broke down the cloistered walls and brought the radical discipleship of the monastic life into the wider Church. Bonhoeffer goes on to use the biography of Luther, himself a monk, who 'escaped the monastery' and attempted to bring the monastic form of discipleship to the entire

---

[104] Dietrich Bonhoeffer, *Discipleship* (Minneapolis: Fortress Press, 2001) p.46-7
[105] Ibid., p.47
[106] Dietrich Bonhoeffer, *Testament to Freedom* (San Francisco: HarperSanFrancisco, 1997) p.424

world.

By the time he reached prison, Bonhoeffer was grasping the implications of this 'new form of monasticism' which was based fully in the world. Part of Bonhoeffer's argument for a 'religionless Christianity' centres on the critique of the un-biblical premise that Christianity is a cosmic escape plan from this world to heaven. In this schema Christianity is a religion interested only in metaphysics and individual salvation. His prison letters to his friend Eberhard Bethge, critiques our modern view of Christianity which desperately attempts to preserve itself against an increasingly forceful argument against the existence of God. In a baptismal homily written for Bethge's son, Bonhoeffer writes,

> Our church, which has been fighting in these years only for its self-preservation, as though that were an end in itself, is incapable of taking the word of reconciliation and redemption to mankind and the world. Our earlier words are therefore bound to lose their force and cease, and our being Christian today will be limited to two things: prayer and righteous action among men. All Christian thinking, speaking, and organizing must be born anew out of this prayer and action.[107]

Whilst we, as God's people, continue to focus on our own survival, perpetuating our own, albeit noble and good activities and arguments, we fail to witness to the power of grace. As we explored in the last chapter, God does come and meet us where we are, but He comes to turn us around, to recalibrate us and for our whole lives to be changed. God does not require us to go seeking Him elsewhere but rather to seek Him in the world to which He is calling us. What is required is that we acknowledge that those noble and good activities may not be achieving the godly purposes we believe they are. This is about continually asking God to direct

---

[107] Bonhoeffer, *Letters and Papers from Prison*, p.105

us and not to presume that once God has given direction we can 'take it from here'.

Imagine standing in the dark unable to see more than a few feet in front of you. You ask God for a light to show you the path. He obliges and lights the next step for you. Most of us, once God has shown us the next step, presume that we know the rest of the path and run off in eagerness, 'following God's call'. In actual fact, we know nothing but the next step. God, in His great wisdom rarely gives long term plans to us, not just because we are unable to grasp such knowledge but because the future doesn't exist.

God has given to us free will to make choices that genuinely change the world in which we live. He is able to hold the infinite possible futures that potentially could unfold but which of those become reality, remains open. It is this limitation of power that is at the heart of God's grace. That is why we must daily return to God to seek His will for the next step. We exist in the world where not everyone chooses to follow God and so the decisions we make will not be always as God intended. The specifics of God's plans, therefore, must change to respond to those other human choices made freely against God's will. Thomas Merton's prayer of abandonment continues to inform my approach to discernment of God's will.

> My Lord God, I have no idea where I am going. I do not see the road ahead of me. I cannot know for certain where it will end. Nor do I really know myself, and the fact that I think I am following your will does not mean that I am actually doing so. But I believe that the desire to please you does in fact please you. And I hope I have that desire in all that I am doing. I hope that I will never do anything apart from that desire. And I know that if I do this, you will lead me by the right road, though I may know nothing about it. Therefore I will trust you always though I may know nothing about it. Therefore I will trust you always though I may seem to be lost and in the shadow of death. I

> will not fear, for you are ever with me, and you will never leave me to face my perils alone.[108]

It is this truth that we must embrace afresh, and we see it profoundly expressed in the crucifixion. We are asked to follow in Jesus' obedience as God improvised through a set narrative, where the end remains the same, the journey adapts.

If we fail to fully grasp this reality, then we are likely to construct a lie around us and live in a fantasy. Thus, attempting to live 'in the world' becomes a retreat from reality as we follow our fictional visions of the future which do not exist. We must commit to the world, in the way God did in Jesus. Thus, faith becomes that reliance on God, looking only to Him to guide and direct us as the landscape and terrain changes. The teleological end to our journey must remain solely in the hands of God as we can, with our penchant for distorted knowledge, imagine the path we must take and, out of fear of realizing the dissonance between our dream and reality, deny reality in favour of fantasy.

> It is not with the beyond that we are concerned, but with this world as created and preserved, subjected to laws, reconciled, and restored. What is above this world is, in the gospel, intended to exist for this world; I mean that, not in the anthropocentric sense of liberal, mystic pietistic, ethical theology, but in the biblical sense of the creation and of the incarnation, crucifixion, and resurrection of Jesus Christ.[109]

What Bonhoeffer is arguing here is that we should be concerned with the world created as it is rather than as we hope it to be. That what lies beyond will be revealed as this world begins to change into it. The purpose of heaven is to shape the earth so that

---

[108] Thomas Meerton, *Thoughts in Solitude* (New York: Farrar, Strauss and Giroux, 1958) p.79
[109] Ibid., p.369-70

it can be, in the end, the Kingdom of God in completeness. The mysterious nature of what that is like is hidden from us, out of the wisdom of God, so we do not distort it with sin.

What has this got to do with baptism? Whilst we continue to allow baptism to be a onetime insurance policy for the afterlife, we deny the power of God's activity in our lives. I think this heaven focused view has all but died out in the Church, but it remains persistent within the folk religion still very prominent in our culture. We, as God's people, must continue to teach the truth of baptism; that baptism is the start of a lifelong pursuit of being increasingly reliant on God. Baptism is the proclamation that we are nothing being made something by God.

> I discovered it is only by living completely in this world that one learns to have faith. One must completely abandon any attempt to make something of oneself, whether it be a saint, or a converted sinner, or a churchman (a so-called priestly type!), a righteous man or an unrighteous one, a sick man or a healthy one. By this-worldliness I mean living unreservedly in life's duties, problems, successes and failures, experiences and perplexities. In doing so we throw ourselves completely into the arms of God, taking seriously, not our own sufferings, but those of God in the world–watching with Christ in Gethsemane. That, I think, is faith; that is metanoia; that is how one becomes human and a Christian.[110]

Baptism, in this understanding, becomes a lifelong commitment to growing in openness to the direction and transformation of ourselves by God. Baptism becomes the public declaration that we know nothing but the grace of God. Baptism becomes a humble desire to have our very identity changed by God

---

[110] Ibid., p137

within the life of the Body of Christ as He redeems us, together, and brings His kingdom to earth.

Christianity is not a spirituality because it forces us to embrace our humanness; the fleshy, tangible life. We are not dualists, yearning for the separation of our souls from our bodies. We are not a people focused on some spiritual nirvana achieved by asceticism or prayerful meditation in the hope of transcending our flesh. We are bodily present, rooted in history and geography, in the world we see, hear and breathe in. The gospel is about the redemption of the world not an escape route from it. Rowan Williams writes, "The only history to be taken seriously is bodily history; and so the redemption of humanity must be located in bodily history."[111]

The beautiful revelation of God through Jesus Christ is that God cares for this world and his eschatological plan is bound up in the atoms and particles of creation. The incarnation is good news for us that our earthly lives are not accidental but have a divine purpose: redemption. It is the religious life, the life of the faithful monks and nuns of old, that should be teaching the wider Church how to live in the hands of our Redeemer as he shapes us into a holy people. It is this way of living that should be at the very heart of Christian discipleship wherever it is lived out.

At baptism preparation I state that baptism/christening makes a child a 'Christian' but then ask parents what it means to be a 'Christian'. Most struggle to define the term, some suggesting that it is a belief in a god. I challenge them by pointing out that most religions believe in a god/gods. In order to open up the conversation I pose the parents a scenario; I ask if their child, when they are 7 or 8 years old, comes up to them and asks,

"Mummy/Daddy, are we Christian?" What would they say? And, if the child then asks, as they are likely to do, "why?" What would the parents' response be?

"Yes. You were christened."

---

[111] Williams, *The Wound Of Knowledge*, p.28

My heart sinks. Rarely do they mention Jesus Christ (despite the clue in the title!) and so I take the opportunity to talk, quite passionately, about being a Christian, about following Jesus, wanting to be transformed into His likeness, to acting, speaking, loving like Jesus, to inviting Him to direct my life, my behaviour and my attitudes. I, like many ministers, comfort myself with the only thing left to us: the 'planting seeds' analogy.

It is not that I don't understand the sowing analogy but I have major theological issues when we're sowing seeds at the point of baptism, our welcoming of new Christians into the Kingdom of God. Infant baptism, for me, relies, in part, on the faith of the parents and/or godparents. Of course, baptism relies on the grace of God and God's relationship with the child but there remain big questions over whether salvation can be removed from someone; can someone turn away from God's grace? It is about free will and choice in the matter of relationship with God. If choice is taken away from baptism then we may as well go round pouring holy water over people and proclaiming faith over them!

> Confession of faith is not to be confused with professing a religion. Such profession uses the confession as propaganda and ammunition against the Godless. The confession of faith belongs rather to the "Discipline of the Secret" in the Christian gathering of those who believe. Nowhere else is it tenable...The primary confession of the Christian before the world is the deed which interprets itself. If this deed is to have become a force, then the world will long to confess the Word. This is not the same as loudly shrieking out propaganda. This Word must be preserved as the most sacred possession of the community. This is a matter between God and the community, not between the community and the world. It is a word of recognition between friends, not a word to use against enemies. This attitude was first learned at baptism. The

deed alone is our confession of faith before the world.[112]

Baptism is not an opportunity to teach people the faith. Baptism must remain the result/ the response to an encounter with the resurrected Jesus in this world. Baptism is the secret admission of another into the community of faith which professes by its prayer and action the reality of God amongst us, reconciling and restoring this world.

The most prominent and profound tension in the trinity of vows (stability, conversion and obedience) begins to emerge as you consider the commitment to stability and to change. A monk is pulled by seemingly opposing forces; one to remain faithful and one to move forward. Under the surface, though, these two vows hold a mysterious unity, a unity that develops as the two dialogue with each other. As you remain faithful to others you will be asked to change. We discover, as we decide to stay, particularly in painful conflict, that the only way that we can maintain stability in our external circumstances is if there is change in our internal circumstance.

We, as Christians, believe pure love is not forceful or manipulative but it must, if it is true love, able to invite the receiver into the freedom to change. We know this by the way God chose to reveal His character in Christ crucified. The change that this love invites in a person is not a deliberate, self-willed change but rather an organic evolution that emerges by looking upon and being looked upon by our Beloved. In this state of self-lessness, i.e. looking outside of our self to an Other, we do not define our self because we are not interested in such a task. We allow ourselves to be defined by the One who truly loves. It's 'not thinking less of yourself' but rather 'thinking of your self less.'[113]

---

[112] Bonhoeffer, *Testament to Freedom*, p.91
[113] Warren, *Purpose Driven Life*, p.186

Such a state of being requires vulnerability because we must risk being without definition, living as a formless void. We must risk the selfless act of openness to others' radical 'seeing' of us, like Solveig of Peer. We must trust in the other to not distort, manipulate or take advantage of our fluctuating, changeable character. We must relinquish control on the other and lay our lives into the others' hand. It takes trust and, as we have seen, this is not something our current culture is good at encouraging or growing, let alone acknowledging its lack.

There is a story of Rabbi Mendel of Kotzk who approached a young man as he ate a fish dish with great glee.

"Why are you eating the fish?" the rabbi asked.

"Because I love fish." replied the man.

"And so, because of your love for fish you have taken it from the water and killed it?" asked the rabbi. "No, you love yourself and because the fish satisfies your own needs you took it out of the water and killed it to eat."[114]

The point of the story is to highlight that much of what we think of as 'love' is 'fish love'. A couple fall in love with each other because they see in one another someone who can satisfy their emotional and physical needs but that is self-focused. It is not love for the other but love of self. This form of love is based on what we receive rather than on what we give. If we stop receiving satisfaction from the person of our affection, we no longer feel we 'love' them. True love is not based on what we receive but on what we give. In giving to another we are investing ourselves in them and we are placing our lives, which we instinctively seek to preserve, in another person. This requires that they are changed by that giving. In turn we must also receive what the other person gives to us which is not necessarily what we would ask for from them. We are changed, therefore by that relationship and by love.

---

[114] found in Abraham J. Twerski, *Happiness and the Human Spirit: the spirituality of becoming the best you can be* (Vermont: Jewish Lights Publishing, 2008) p.76-77

Stability, therefore, is required in order for change to occur. Conversion is required in order for us to stay. For the unity of these two, seemingly competing vows to be fully realised, however, we must add to them a third dimension; that of obedience. It is the vow of obedience which holds and unifies the other two as it calls us to release control and power over ourselves and invites us into relationship with others. In this way we begin to see how the dynamic interaction between these three vows can encourage the development of an inner environment necessary to grow in real, Christ-like love.

Study

If you profit from it, therefore, read with humility, simplicity and faith, and never seek a reputation for being learned. Seek willingly and listen attentively to the words of the saints.[115]

To participate in the Church requires an intentional, ongoing metanoia and kenosis following the lived example of Jesus. This emptying of self is done, as we explored in our chapter on prayer, in the hope of being filled with the Spirit of Christ which will transform us into His likeness. In the posture of prayer we seek God but not in some spiritual ecstatic experience but in the reality of our lives. In Jesus, God entered our physical reality to find us, wash us from the stain of sin and lead us to the freedom of a new life in Him. He does not force or impose that change on us but attempts to woo us back into relationship with Him. God does not hide in a fantasy to which we must escape to in order to encounter Him but He continues to make Himself visible in reality. If God exists, He must exist in the actuality of our world and experience. It is here, therefore, that we must search for Him and that search begins with prayer, as outlined before, but also in intentional study of God's creation; a seeking for Him where He may be found.

Evagrius's three-stage formation of discipleship should not be read as a sequence of separate activities; rather it is a layering of habits that directs a person towards the spiritual life. In his treatise 'Chapters on Prayer', he writes, "If you are a theologian, you pray truly, and if you pray truly you are a theologian."[116] It is this rooting in prayer which gives life and context for the discovery of

---

[115] Thomas a Kempsis, *The Imitation of Christ* (New York: Dover Publications, 2012) p.5
[116] Sr. Pascale-Dominique Nau (tr.), *Evagrius Ponticus' Chapters on Prayer, Ch 60* (Rome: Sr. Pascale-Dominique Nau, 2012)

the character of God and of His will. The practices of study that enable us to discover the way, the truth and the life of God must be done in the posture of prayer rooted in the very reality of our existence. I will be using the term 'study' to not only mean the reading of written texts but any physical vehicle God might use to communicate His character and purposes which, we will discover, are various.

Every journey must consist of moving towards one place and this requires moving away from another. In this way every journey requires an element of change or conversion. We started our journey with the liturgical refrain 'remember you are dust and to dust you shall return. Turn away from sin and be faithful to Christ.'[117] We must, however, move on, through the water of baptism and proclaim: 'You have been clothed with Christ. As many as are baptized into Christ have put on Christ.'[118] This statement is both a present reality and a future hope, for although we commit our lives into the person of Christ, we acknowledge that it is also a process of transformation. As we journey towards God we move away from a life without God and so, redemption is not merely a gift bestowed upon us but a process we engage in. Study/learning is the active engagement in this process of moving from our acknowledged nothingness without God to being made something by our 'putting on of Christ'.

"For many of us," Brian C. Taylor observes, "learning is something we do all at once at a particular time in our youth." He goes on,

> Education becomes a mere tool to get us toward the goal of a good job, the favour of our parents, or social acceptability. Daily study, on the other hand, because it

[117] The Archbishops' Council, *Times and Seasons*, p.230

[118] The Archbishops' Council, *Common Worship: Christian Initiation* (London: Church House Publishing, 2006) p. 71

> takes place slowly and consistently over time, gives us the much more desirable goal of becoming an integrated person in God.[119]

St Paul insists on the experience of transformation in the life of disciples of Christ.

> Do not be conformed to this world, but be transformed by the renewing of your minds, so that you may discern what is the will of God – what is good and acceptable and perfect. (Rom 12:2)

St Paul uses the same word for 'transformed', μεταμορφόω (*metamorphoo*), as the gospel writers use to describe Jesus being 'transfigured'. The difference with St Paul's use of the word and the gospel writers' use in the event of the Transfiguration is that this verb is in the present tense, ie. it is an ongoing process. Our transformation is not a onetime event in history (unlike Jesus') but a process of change. Due to our addiction to sin we are likely to re-turn to the old life, heading back in the wrong direction. The water of baptism which washes off the stains of sin is the start of our continual conversion outlined in the last chapter.

The other grammatical interest in the use of *metamorphoo* is it highlights that we are the passive object in this activity. Our transformation implies we are not the catalyst or agent for change. In practice this does not mean that we have no agency at all in the process but rather we must actively place ourselves into the hands of the true agent of change; God. We do this, so St Paul suggests, by 'the renewal of our minds' and the word he uses for 'mind' is νοός (*nous*). *Nous* is often the vehicle through which we drive our will. St Paul is thus arguing that by making new our mind (recalibrating it) we can then know, discern, experience the will of

[119] Taylor, Spirituality for Everyday Life, p.39

God rather than just our own. In other words, we can clear out the vehicle of our will to make room for God's will to be let in.

The heresy of Monothelitism is the belief that Jesus, despite having two natures only has one will which is divine. At the heart of this heresy is the view that the human will, at its basic level, will always be in complete opposition to the divine will. In order for Jesus to always do what His heavenly Father wills means that He needed to give up His human will and desires. If we accept this view, then the transformation spoken of in the New Testament requires a slaying of our human will and freedom of choice in order to be enslaved to God. Jonathan Mitchican, a Catholic priest in Texas, wrote a brilliant article on this subject. He argued that there is a 'reigning notion of freedom in Western society today.'

> Freedom is synonymous with a lack of restriction. It means having complete control. The person who must do the will of another — such as an employee or a child or a slave — is not free. The person who must conform to some kind of standard outside of himself, be it moral or social or simply aesthetic, is effectively in bondage.[120]

That is, however, not what is depicted in the person of Jesus. Jesus calls us to be His disciples and to learn from Him how to be human. We will never be able to possess a divine will; that's not what we were created for. We were created with free human wills. Jesus came to live a human life to show us how to be what we were created to be. Rather than trying to eradicate the gift of free will, God is redeeming that gift by calling us to train our wills to imitate that of the divine will. God created us to be like Him in our wills and, therefore, we are truly free when we learn to live within that truth. As we saw earlier, Rowan Williams stated the image of God

[120] Jonathan Mitchican, "The Greatest Heresy Of Our Time Isn't what You Think It Is", https://livingchurch.org/covenant/2016/10/17/the-greatest-heresy-of-our-time-isnt-what-you-think/

'must be made into a 'likeness' by the exercise of goodness.' It is this practice of deliberately exercising our wills to follow that of Jesus' human will that we find ourselves being made into the likeness of God's divine will. Again, we are seeking theonomy, the freely chosen receipt of the freely offered gift of God's will for us.

Richard Foster, in his excellent book 'Celebration of Discipline', talks about study as a spiritual discipline and begins his chapter exploring it by stating, "the apostle Paul tells us that we are transformed through the renewal of the mind (Rom 12:2). The mind is renewed by applying it to those things that will transform it."

> 'Finally brethren, whatever is true, whatever is honourable, whatever is just, whatever is pure, whatever is lovely, whatever is gracious, if there is any excellence, if there is anything worthy of praise, think about these things' (Phil 4:8). The Discipline of Study is the primary vehicle to bring us to 'think about these things.' [121]

Scripture is the inspired account of God's revelation of Himself to His people throughout human history. It is the shared narrative that gives shape to our interpretation of existence and points us towards the eschatological character we are being called towards, embodied in the person of Jesus Christ. Without it, we are forced to make up our own narrative and return to the masks that hide us from truly knowing ourselves.

To study Scripture is to inhabit the story we were made for, to learn our part and rehearse our character, clothed in the costume of Christ. This study is not to be a mere memorizing of fact or possession of knowledge but a rendering of ourselves by the story. The reason Scripture is authoritative to a Christian community is because it contains all that is true, honourable, just, pure, etc. and so gives the ordered framework which holds and shapes our lives.

---

[121] Foster, *Celebration of Discipline*, p.78

In the very act of retelling of the story of Scripture we learn what it means to be God's people.

> How is it possible that the gospel should be credible, that people should come to believe that the power which has the last word in human affairs is represented by a man hanging on a cross? I am suggesting that the only answer, the only hermeneutic of the Gospel is a congregation of men and women who believe it and live by it.... Its character is given to it, when it is true to its nature, not by the characters of its members but by his character. Insofar as it is true to its calling, it becomes the place where men and women and children find that the gospel gives them the framework of understanding, the "lenses" through which they are able to understand and cope with the world.[122]

To return to Evagrius' threefold process of development in the spiritual life; after the 'prakitke', or stripping of our own understanding and worldview, he proposes that one applies the mind to contemplate Scripture and nature in search of God's wisdom.

> Theoria physike, Evagrius' version of natural philosophy, means for him the contemplation of the natural world and of the Scriptures, by means of which the monk was to apply his nous, which had been rehabilitated by asceticism, to the divine wisdom which Evagrius held to have been deposited in the Scripture and in creation.[123]

Foster agrees with this approach postulating that,

---

[122] Leslie Newbigin, *The Gospel in a Pluralist* Society (London: SPCK, 2004) p.227
[123] Stefaniw, "Exegetical Curricula in Origen, Didymus, and Evagrius", p.288

> In study there are two books to be studied: verbal and non verbal. Books and lectures, therefore constitute only half the field of study, perhaps less. The world of nature and, most important, the careful observation of events and actions are the primary non verbal fields of study.[124]

If God has entered our world in order to redeem, not just our spirits but our flesh and, indeed, all of creation, then we must look for what is true, honourable, just, pure, etc. in creation. God created the physical world and nature and He is redeeming it too. We could easily escape reality by entering into the Scriptural world, divorcing ourselves from creation. God calls us to seek Him in the world, too. He uses Scripture, however, to indicate how to do that.

Hugh of St Victor was an Augustinian Canon Regular in the 12th century whose book 'Didascalicon' is a beautiful and systematic framework for sacred learning. Life, for Hugh, was for the 'construction of a dwelling place, an *aedificato* for the presence of God within human persons,' and this is done, 'through their reformation in the image of God, accomplished through ordered practices.'[125] Hugh writes,

> The subject of all of divine Scripture is the work of restoration for humanity. There are two works in which all this is done. The first is the work of creation. The second is the work of restoration.[126]

In an account of the Creation narrative Hugh writes,

---

[124] Foster, *Celebration of Discipline*, p.80
[125] Boyd Coolman, *The Theology of Hugh of St. Victor: an interpretation* (Cambridge: Cambridge University Press, 2010), p.3
[126] Hugh of St Victor, *De Sacramentis Christianae Fidei* (Patrologiae cursus completus (PL) 176.183A)

> ...in the rational creature, being was made first, and afterwards beautiful or lovely being: something better was to be added, so that the rational creature would not glory too much in the good which it had first accepted, but instead would hasten to the better thing he was going to receive afterwards.[127]

This work to build a beautiful, ordered dwelling out of the soul for the Divine to inhabit is not of human effort but rather of God. The encounter with the Holy for Hugh is both a departure and a destination which causes him to write that 'He will come to you in order to make a dwelling place in you. For He does not find it when He comes; rather He comes in order to build. First He constructs, afterward He indwells.'[128]

The intention of reading Scripture, in the ordered way prescribed by Hugh, is to allow God to re-form the reader. This practice aims to combine the concrete and 'visible' with the spiritually abstract. The study of Scripture is a two-fold reading; one, a mental exercise in gathering and retaining historical information and, two, as 'an object of extended, theological meditation.'[129] Hugh concludes that 'the start of learning, thus, lies in reading, but its consummation lies in meditation.'[130]

Hugh places significant importance on recollection of data but it is never his desired destination but rather a step along the way, indeed it is only the foundation. Hugh repeats, throughout his work, a threefold analogy of construction; 'first the foundation is laid, then the structure is raised upon it, and finally, when the work is all finished, the house is decorated by the laying on of color.'[131] In 'Didascalicon' he details what each layer represents, beginning

---

[127] Hugh of St Victor, *Miscellanae 1.48* (PL 177.497B)
[128] Hugh of St Victor, *De Quinque Septenis* (PL175.411A)
[129] Coolman, *Theology of Hugh of St Victor*, p. 18
[130] Hugh of St Victor, Jerome Taylor (ed. and trans.), *The Didascalicon of Hugh of St Victor: a medieval guide to the arts*, 3:10 (New York: Columbia University Press, 1961)
[131] Hugh of St Victor, *Didascalicon* 6.2

with the learning of history which takes on a broader category than the modern mind understands of it. Hugh commends to his students, 'learn everything; you will see afterwards that nothing is superfluous.'[132] Part of Hugh's theological aim is to systematically construct a comprehensive programme of reading/studying the created world as the means of knowing God but the correct interpretation of it is found through reason taking in faith, morals and contemplation.

After the foundation is laid, the student must then explore the allegorical meaning of what has been learnt working through things they find obscure, things they find clear and things they find doubtful. If they conform to 'what you ought unquestionably to profess and truthfully to believe' then they are to be placed orderly in the symbolic building; if not, turn them over further and discern their purpose. This process is the meditation on the Word of God but equally on the Church Fathers and Mothers. This meditation 'provides counsel'[133] so that knowledge is used to improve the person rather than remain wasted.

Hugh's theology is a theology of reformation done by God in the individual through the structured process of learning. It is an ordered activity in the gathering and understanding of creation in order 'to restore within us the divine likeness, a likeness which is to us a form, but to God is his nature.'[134] This likeness of the Divine is best seen in the person of Jesus Christ, the Redeemer, who is also the personification of Wisdom. Wisdom in the Augustinian tradition is synonymous with Christ as a remedy to fallen humanity. This gives the reason, for Hugh, as to why God became man.

We are baptized into the communal Body of Christ and begin a life of discipleship; a life-long learning to follow Jesus and being transformed into His likeness. In order to follow Jesus we must first

---

[132] Hugh of St Victor, *Didascalicon* 6.3
[133] Hugh of St Victor, *Didascalicon* 5.9
[134] Hugh of St Victor, *Didascalicon* 2.1

know Him and in order to know Him we must first see Him as He is and we do that by reading the accounts of His life in Scripture, not just the gospels but the whole of the story of God. Having acknowledged, by the gift of faith, that God has made Himself known to us in Jesus, we must then continue to allow the reality of the resurrected Christ remain independent from our imagination. What I mean by that is Jesus must not become as we want Him to be. Jesus must shape us, not us shape Him. Discipleship, in part, therefore, is a process of identifying blind spots in our vision and understanding of Scripture and the character of God revealed within it. Our study is always vulnerable to this kind of error when done on our own because one cannot know what isn't seen without someone else telling us. The study of Scripture, if it is going to be truly transformative in any way, must be rooted in a community. Rooted by a humility that comes from acknowledging who we are in relation to God and His creation and a stability that holds us in a place through difficulty and challenge.

When it comes to the important work of learning from one another and being in a community of study, we begin with this very question that Rowan Williams suggests,

> …the first thing we ought to think of when in the presence of another Christian individual or Christian community is: what is Christ giving me through this person, this group?[135]

At Pentecost, God poured out His Holy Spirit onto all those who turned to Him in faith. St. Peter announced to all those gathered that this was the fulfillment of a promise made by God through the prophet Joel,

> In the last days it will be, God declares, that I will pour out my Spirit upon all flesh, and your sons and your daughters

---

[135] Rowan Williams, Being Disciples () p. 8

> shall prophesy, and your young men shall see visions, and your old men shall dream dreams. Even upon my slaves, both men and women, in those days I will pour out my Spirit… Then everyone who calls on the name of the Lord shall be saved. (Acts 2:17-18, 21)

Here, at the birth of the Church, God was beginning communal prophecy. Prophecy in Scripture is the speaking of hidden things, not a soothsaying or fortune telling. A prophet is someone who knows the mind/will of God and speaks it for others to hear. At Pentecost that prophetic task became a shared task for all God's people; everyone was able to hear from God. The necessary task of discerning the voice of God became a corporate activity. Visions were tested against dreams and the Church became a place where all were to seek the gift of prophecy (knowing the mind/will of God).

The testing of prophecy has been a dynamic struggle ever since. Even in the Early Church, as seen in the writings of St. Paul, it is not clear as to how the Church should agree on interpretation. Jürgen Moltmann outlines three different paradigms of the Church throughout history: The Hierarchical paradigm of God the Father, the Christocentric paradigm of God the Son and the Charismatic paradigm of God the Spirit. He suggests that in the Early Church there was a monarchic social structure seen through the authority of the Father and manifested itself in Apostolic teaching which grew into Papal supremacy. This caused a social rebellion in the form of the Reformation, which replaced such a view with a brotherhood of believers based on the centrality of sola scriptura. Moltmann admits, 'Of course, practically speaking the distinction between trained theologians and people without any theological training has taken the place of priestly hierarchy.'[136]

[136] Jürgen Moltmann, *Sun of Righteousness, Arise! God's Future for Humanity and the Earth* (Minneapolis: Fortress Press, 2010) p23

In the last of these paradigms, it is God the Spirit that brings unity whilst encouraging plurality. In the charismatic congregation, Moltmann suggests, 'no one has a higher or lower position than anyone else with what he or she can contribute to the community, all are accepted just as they are.'[137] There remains significant challenges to this paradigm, like the other two, around the issue of authority which we will explore later. For now, it is enough to use the progression of these paradigms to draw out important ecclesiological aspects to hold onto from each to encourage discipleship.

The Hierarchical paradigm had the security of stability. Jesus' teaching was passed down by agreed upon sources and people judged what was true, good and right by that set standard. The Christocentric paradigm had the emphasis on personal conversion. People were encouraged to learn, for themselves, the teachings of Jesus found in Scripture and to apply it to their personal lives. The Charismatic paradigm has the potential of holding a community together through shared obedience. Our distortions of Jesus' teaching can be tested against others' view as we discern together what it means to be like Jesus.

Through the water of baptism and by the ongoing life of discipleship we are clothing ourselves with Christ and we should expect to witness transformation of our lives. We will begin, as we journey on, to reflect more and more of His glory and others should be able to see in us, something of the person of Christ. We should become walking revelations of God's activity in the world. We should become texts to be studied by others in order to know what God is like. It is in our very bodies and lived realities that Christ is re-embodied in the world by the power and work of His Spirit working in us.

> He that studies only men, will get the body of knowledge without the soul; and he that studies only books, the soul

[137] Ibid.

> without the body. He that to what he sees adds observation, and to what he reads, reflection is in the right road to knowledge, provided that in scrutinising the hearts of others, he neglects not his own.[138]

The call to engage in study is to ensure that we continue to engage in reality as it is. The challenges of community, the difficulties of dialogue are there to root us in what is real, so we don't get high on our fantasies. The struggle required, at times, should prompt us to remember the work of God in our redemption through Christ. We need to renew our minds to keep our emotions in check. Richard Foster warns,

> Good feelings will not free us. Ecstatic experiences will not free us. Getting 'high on Jesus' will not free us. Without a knowledge of the truth, we will not be free.[139]

In his exploration of living in community, Jean Vanier, expresses the joys and the challenges that any of us who have dared to engage in real community can witness to. There is, he suggests, an initial rush of euphoria when one tastes something of the communion for which we are made. After people 'lift their masks and become vulnerable, they discover that community can be a terrible place, because it is a place of relationship'

> ...it is the revelation of our wounded emotions and of how painful it can be to live with others, especially with some people. It is so much easier to live with books and objects, television, or dogs and cats! It is so much easier to live

---

[138] Caleb Cotton, *Lacon or Many Things In Few Words Addressed To Those Who Think*, Vol.II.CLX (London:Longman, Orme, Brown, Green and Longmans, 1837) p.115
[139] Foster, *Celebration of Discipline*, p. 79

> alone and just do things for others, when one feels like it.'[140]

The importance of communal study, therefore, is to learn to learn together. The purpose of study is to be changed by that which is not you in the safety of stable relationship.

If the life of faith is like a journey then, like the woman in the parable, we need to find ways of finding the help we need and following the guide. It is by knowing and following the will of God that we are led to our teleological end, the destination for which we were created: pure communion with God Himself as part of His Body. God communicates His will to us through many different mediums; the Scriptures, the lives and writings of the saints through history, the experience of other disciples in community and, indeed in the everyday 'coincidences' or events of life. The practice of study is merely the open reception of these things with the intention of filling our mind and lives with the love and knowledge of God.

> All study, if it is to be worth anything at all, must find its way into the core of our spiritual being where God can integrate the learning and transform us by his grace.'[141]

[140] Jean Vanier, *Community and Growth* (New York: Paulist Press, 1989) p. 25
[141] Taylor, *Spirituality for Everyday Living*, p.39

OIL

Sanctification

The Kingdom of God is like a manager coming to check on a tenant farmer...[142]

How do we hold onto something without becoming possessive over it? How do we care for a precious gift whilst sharing it freely with others? How do we resist the temptation to constrict and label without losing distinction and diversity? Everything is not the same. There are categories of existence; a cat is not a dog, I am not you, good is not evil.

It is like a manager coming to check on one of his farms. His trust of the farmers under his supervision knows no bounds. His leadership style is very permissive and egalitarian. He respects the wisdom of the men and women below him.

After a morning walking round one farm where the sheep are crammed into a field not large enough to house the dwindling flock. The farmer reached capacity some years past but hasn't had the resources to gain more land and so the sheep have suffered. The farmer has worked hard to try and solve this complex problem.

Tired and frustrated, the manager is keen to see his next farm to see how they manage to increase in sheep season upon season. He drives up the winding driveway to the farmhouse where the farmer who ran the property and kept the sheep sits awaiting his manager. As the manager approaches the farmer stands to welcome him to the homestead.

Unlike the previous farmer this man is calm and serene. He has no concerns or on the lookout for any scrap of space to put another sheep, he has time to look out on his flock and appreciate the

[142] This story is not my own. I first heard it from a friend, who heard it from a friend, who heard it from a friend, *ad nausum*. I am unable to source the original teller; if it is you, I thank you.

scenery and the wonder and abundance of creation that surrounds him.

"Greetings, brother," the manager calls, "How goes your day?"

"Beautiful, isn't it?" the farmer replies.

"We've been blessed in these parts with good health and increased numbers of sheep."

"Have we, indeed?" the farmer responds, almost naive to the good fortune.

"Have you not seen an increase here?" the manager asks nervously.

"We continue to see many beautiful specimens and rejoice over the flock."

The manager is becoming increasingly concerned about the farmer's lack of commitment and is now eager to check on the farm. Maybe he, as the manager, has given too much freedom to this farmer; maybe he has misplaced his trust in the competency and wisdom of this worker. The farmer, however, stands serenely gazing out at the fields.

"You are free to explore the acres of land and bring back your report of what you see and find." With those words the farmer takes a seat and lifts the glass of water to his lips.

The manager sets out, bemused by the farmer, to walk the grounds that sprawl into the horizon. The map he has in his records marking out the territory of this farm is confused and vague. As he explores the land he returns again and again to try and figure out what the remit of his oversight is. Nonetheless, he checks the quality of the grass as he goes and he counts sheep whenever he finds them. Having not fallen asleep after such an exercise he makes random spot checks on the quality of the meat and the health of the animals.

What he views is very good and he is impressed with the farmer's care and clearly profitable oversight of his treasures. The sheep are healthy, happy and safe, the grass and grounds are well kept and free of chemicals. How does he manage to keep the sheep so well with so little work?

The light begins to fade and yet the manager still isn't clear as to which parts were under the care of the farmer and which weren't. If the map was anything to go by then this farmer had performed a miracle because whenever the manager thought he'd got to the parameters and limits of the farm he found another field, seemingly classified as his. After a long afternoon he returns to the farmhouse to meet with the farmer.

"It's all very impressive." The manager says, "The sheep are healthy and you have many ready for market. There is one thing, which troubles me... You don't have any fences. Your land seems to just continue to spread far and wide and there's no visible demarcation to the neighbouring farmers' lands. How do you keep all your sheep together and close by?"

The farmer smiles. He leans close to the manager to tell his secret,

"We dig very deep wells."

This popular story opens up a great deal of reflection as we consider how God gathers and cares for His people. From the call of Abraham to the exile from Jerusalem the narrative of God's people is an account of exclusion and tribal protection. This is often criticised by Christians who, as a predominantly Gentile based Jewish movement, misunderstand or overlook the necessity of the early formation of communal identity for the Israelites.

God's plan of redemption in the Old Testament had to begin somewhere and, if God does not force people to turn to Him, this means there was always going to be some who did not identify themselves with Him. Built into the freedom of choice is the inherent exclusion and tribalism that some baulk at. God chooses some and not others by means of the consequence of free will and not in some petty-minded, arbitrary whim. He accepts that some may not choose to listen or follow, He remains committed to them, but that commitment won't be reciprocated. God's choice of one group over another, therefore, is based on the foundational choice to give His creatures free will.

There's a repeated image throughout the history of God and His children of landlord and tenant. The phrase, "I shall be their God and they shall be my people", or versions of it, occur 28 times in the Bible; the covenant with Abraham (Genesis 17:7-8), the covenant with Moses (Exodus 6:7), the covenant with the Israelites (e.g. Leviticus 26:11-12), the covenant with David as King (2 Samuel 7:24) and into the prophetic era with Jeremiah, Ezekiel, et al. (e.g. Jeremiah 32:38, Ezekiel 11:20)

The children of God found themselves oppressed by an empire and turned to the Father for help. He heard the cries of His poor people and promised to lead them out of slavery to freedom. He asked for their obedience and they were willing to do anything to be freed from repression. He overthrew the human dictatorship through the miraculous; He opened up the logic of His rule on fallible and limited human rulers. His people followed Him into a wide-open space on their way to enter a Promised Land.

On the way, however, the children are tempted again to return to their old ways. They believed they could organise themselves and survive without God telling them what to do. In this way the obedience demanded from them felt constrictive and oppressive and they began to grumble.

"We've just replaced one authoritarian despot for another," they said, "At least back then we had comfort and food." Freedom is not as pleasurable as we imagine it. We speak of freedom but in the last assessment we're addicted to our chains. Freedom requires choice, whereas in slavery the difficulty of choice is stripped from us and we're given the freedom to complain internally about the consequences of choices made for us.

Once the children of God were back with their loving Father and He was showing them again what freedom was really like, they panicked. They were not used to living like this; where choices they made had consequences which they could not hide from or blame others for, where they were aware of their own reliance on earthly pleasures and where they were faced with their petty weaknesses and deeply held but distorted prejudices against others. It was in the wide-open space of freedom that choices meant temptations and they were being asked to choose again: 'trust God or take control?'

In grumbling, the children of God vocalised the internal choice they had made: to question God's plans and God's capabilities to help them. To them, God needed their help, as He clearly didn't know where He was going. For God it was just like the garden at the beginning. The healing of this addiction to self-reliance and self-delusion was going to take more drastic measures. God was going to need to take His children through cold turkey.

He led them through the wilderness for 40 years to show them, repeatedly, that He could provide, that He could be trusted, that they could be reformed and redeemed. He was going to show them how obedience could lead them to a life of real freedom and their choices would become in line with His choices. In short, God was going to take His children through a rehearsal period to learn the real character and the narrative in which He wanted them to inhabit.

Before the people of God entered this new land and began to work out what it meant to choose God and not their human temptations they required some boundaries and structuring to, not only mark them out as 'holy'/separate; perpetual blood on their metaphorical doorposts, as it were, but also to protect themselves from outside temptations. Along with the traditional, 'Hebrew' people (the people who had known of God for centuries) there was a 'mixed multitude' (Exodus 12:38), other people from the lower strata of Egyptian society. To unite this 'multitude', this rag-tag rabble required some identity markings.

Circumcision had always been a covenantal symbol for the Hebrews but had become just a rite of passage. That one act, done before one could remember (most of the time), did not bear the fruit of obedience. If they were going to stand on their own two feet and look to God for authority and governance, they needed more than an aesthetic they need something internal.

Moses, one who truly sought to obey God, was asked to implement a training programme. This 'law' given in the wilderness was like a cast put around a broken limb; if it is not put on then the breakage doesn't fix. The law held the people together when there was a great danger of further damage being done. It became, for the people, a safety fence. If someone strayed outside of it, they would likely become infected again by the outside and bring back the infection into the rest of the community. To discern whether you were part of the community of God, or not, depended on your acceptance and observance of the Law of Moses. So, as well as classifying the Israelites, the Law was also self-protective. If you didn't want to stray from the more central tenants of it, there were helpful commandments to encourage you to obey and remain within the protection and grouping of the clan. All of these helped the people to know who God was and how to respond to Him but also to know that they were part of the family.

As nomads, the people of God, in the wilderness, had no fixed residency, no property. They lived in tents and ate what they found lying on the ground (gifts from God!) This made them feel vulnerable and it was this that caused them to turn away from God. It was fear that led them to store food when they were told they didn't need to. Fear turned to self-protection, which in turn transformed into greed and self-sufficiency rules the heart.

Our culture has fallen prey to this series of events, and it all begins with fear. Fear is the driving force of most of the issues in the world; is it any wonder God is so keen to stress, "Do not fear." This phrase, or versions of it, occurs 64 times through the Bible. When we feel vulnerable and our sense of survival is put in question, we build walls, barriers to protect us. We cut ourselves off from threat and, before we know it, we don't trust anyone and so we must rely on ourselves.

As humans we tend to favour defining and designating the outskirts of our territory by boundaries and borders. We build city walls, we argue over territorial boundaries, we look out and see the limits of our span of interaction. Walls also act as protection from 'outsiders'; those who are not part of our community; those who are different, other, and alien.

A group that deliberately chooses to have no boundaries, borders or barriers is un-fearful of those who are not part of the community; they need no defense or protection from 'outsiders'. They seem to exist with a view that those who are different are in no way a threat, but could it be more than this though? Could the lack of walls, in some way, destroy the concept of 'outsiders' completely?

The concept of 'community' is a rhetorical winner in the modern age. In politics and social construction, it is assumed that 'community' is a universally desired entity and should be protected, upheld and promoted. Over the centuries it has, however, become a term with multiple facets and definitions to the extent it is impossible to assume that another shares one's concept of community. It has so many sub-abstractions that, trying to define this beautiful, intuitive experience, it is increasingly difficult without it becoming clinical and dry. It has, as a term, become somewhat vacuous by its overuse.

Community and social groupings fascinate me. I love looking at the organic, complex systems of human interaction. I used to live in a place where there had been, over the decades, a subtle erosion of 'community spirit'. I heard stories from all over the area of 'how it used to be'. Nostalgia is a dangerous thing when left un-challenged but even with an element of skepticism these stories can be truly felt, and the loss is deep.

It is not alone in this experience. Across the UK there's been a loss of those support networks, the intuitive, protective relationships that exist between one person and another. Families live apart, people do not exist in a local context due to the increase of the 'global village', we are encouraged to look after ourselves and, as we accumulate more possessions, our homes really become our castles.

There's a strange story in the book of Genesis. After Noah and the disaster of the flood, people found themselves in a place called Shinar[143] where they began the task of rebuilding. This construction work could not be limited to architecture, although that would be important; no, this work needed to get to the heart of their existence. Social management, priorities, values and character, these were the topics of conversation, or at least they should have been. It was the deep and complex work of discerning what would be the governing principles under which this new society would live which would have been prioritized.

A great, productive system of politics emerged where everyone was on the same page, they all spoke a common language, they understood each other, they shared a common purpose, and everyone did their part. This nation was progressing, and progress, reward, luxury and order were the marks of success. Doing more, doing better, these were the goals; bigger, faster, easier. Never had so much been invented and discovered. If a problem arose, they would find a solution and solve the issue.

They were all of one heart and mind and they shared everything in common.

When humanity looked back to before the flood, they acknowledged that it was the disparity and self-seeking ambition that drove their forefathers to opulence and depravity. Their ancestors were only interested in satisfying their base, self-seeking desires. Humanity had grown up and learnt from that mistake; now they were sophisticated, controlled. The selfish indulgences of the

---

[143] Shinar is thought to have been what we now know as Babylonia. The Babylonian Empire, for the author of Genesis 11 was the example of civilisation, progress and power. The name derived from the Hebrew for 'two rivers' which were identified as the Tigris and Euphrates rivers in Western Asia and Mesopotamia. It was highly fertile and made it a natural centre of trade and commerce and the beginnings of the Babylonian Empire.

past were gone, now were the days of planning, personal restraint and progress.

The success and growth of the nation relied on every man, woman and child playing their part in the objectives of the whole society. This was a big society and it required each one to play its part. Responsibility was needed; no more going at it alone. The mandate was, 'we're all in it together' and together they could build the future, they could become great in the eyes of everyone.

This is an image of what we seem to want to achieve in the West today: peaceful co-habitation, acceptance of all in plurality. In Shinar, we discovered that harmonious living is, for whatever reason, a desirable thing; peace, it seems, has always been our prayer. But we attempted something in Shinar that may help us to define a community in a radically inventive way. Out of boredom, if nothing else, we decided to build a bigger dwelling to encompass more people, but we did not build walls, we built a tower at the centre. The fact we built a tower and not a wall is ingenious and distinctive.

A community, at its most simple level, is a collective descriptor of a group of living organisms, usually humans, who share a commonality, but this highlights an implicit assumption that there is a division between the individual parts. One cannot talk about community without talking, in some sense, in plurality; the desire to be one is undeniable but go into more detail and it is inescapable that it takes more than one person to make a community. Unity becomes a 'oneness' shared by a multiple. A community is a unified group of individual parts.

This has led some to emphasize the boundaries of community; they look at the perceived distinction of a community from the larger society in which they exist, i.e. what is it that unites this group of individuals compared with others? This is perfectly valid.

Stanley Hauerwas begins his book 'Community of Character' clearly defining his aim 'to reassert the social significance of the church as a distinctive society with an integrity peculiar to itself.'[144]

As Christian communities, we often define ourselves and draw attention to our 'us and them' mentality. Mission has become synonymous with 'going out' but out from where? Out from the internally defined limits of our community? We want to talk to those *outside* the Church. We want to go to *them*. All this betrays our perception and acceptance of our boundaries. God calls his people to be 'holy' (1 Pet 1:16), 'sanctified' (Jn 17:15-19), to 'not be conformed to this world.' (Rom 12:2). I want to repeat Shane Claiborne's hope for God's people,

> …Jesus calls us to be peculiar but also to engage in the world we find ourselves in. We are to be relevant nonconformists. We are to develop countercultural habits and norms (the Sermon on the Mount) and live them in the midst of an insane world. Much of the church, however, in its search for relevance, falls in love with the world, its methods of communication, and its patterns of consumerism, and sacrifices holy nonconformity for the sake of cultural relevancy.[145]

Rt Rev. John Thomson phrases it in a similar way,

> Sometimes being odd in a sinful world is one of the gifts of the church to that world. It indicates that this gathering is on God's terms rather than being determined by human choice. As such it witnesses to God's effect upon the church.[146]

So what does it mean to be 'holy'?

---

[144] Hauerwas, *Community of Character*, p.1
[145] Shane Claiborne, *Jesus for President*, p. 238-240
[146] John B Thomson, Sharing Friendship: exploring Anglican character, vocation, witness and mission (Surrey: Ashgate, 2015) p.40

'Holy' comes from the Germanic languages of the Viking and Saxons and was used to mean those things set apart or 'sanctified' for use by the gods. It was used in translations for the Latin word 'sanctus' from which we get the word 'sanctification'. In the Bible, the Greek word most often translated into 'holy' is ἅγιος (*hagios*) or the verb variation ἁγιάζω (*hagiazo*) which means to purify, to clean, to separate from profane things. Holiness, therefore, is about separateness from 'profane things', there is an intrinsic division between things that are holy and things that are not. God's people are called to be distinct, separate, not identified as the same as other things. These boundaries between God's people and those who have freely chosen not to be a part will always exist because otherwise we undermine the choice to not identify with God and it is God, in the Hebrew Scriptures, that defines 'holiness'. It is God alone whose being and essence is 'holy', all holy things/places/times are holy because they relate to or are identified with God who is holiness. God gives things their holiness as a gift of grace.

God's relationship with people makes them holy, different from those who do not have that relationship. This holiness should be made manifest and visible as people live a different way of life to others and so, the Church, the collective noun for these holy people, is called to be a visible sign of the Kingdom of God active in the world.

> For Hauerwas, the embodiment of the church in its micro performances is critical to its mission and witness. This is where sanctification is visible, a redeemed baptismal anthropology which acts as the primary witness of the pilgrim church.[147]

In baptism we are washed clean, set apart and immediately are identified as 'holy', alongside fellow 'holy' people. In this

---

[147] Ibid., p.13

identification, which is based solely on our relationship with Holiness itself, we acknowledge there is a demarcation of certain people; there is a boundary dividing those who are in relationship with God and those who are not. We pass over the threshold, walk through the gate, only when we identify ourselves with the Holy God, but we pass through nonetheless. How we relate to those boundaries and articulate them, however, is key.

In building a tower in Shinar, rather than walls, the 'them' was destroyed by the lack of distinction. This community was defined by something other than its boundaries, and the difficulty of entering this community, of passing through a daunting threshold, was abolished by the destruction of the concept of walls. All were welcome. Before we completely deconstruct the concept of 'walls' we must remember that they do more than keep enemies out; they also keep people in.

We are all a mass of contradictions and paradoxes held together by forces unknown pulling us in different directions. For a creature, in this rational culture, so bent on integrity and certainty, it is an endless frustration that we remain so conflicted, illogic in its purest form. One could say the source of so much division in society is the war going on in each of us as we try to balance the equation of our identity. We blame forces outside of ourselves when, in actual fact, it is more likely the inner turmoil causing us distress. Thomas Merton once described it in this way,

> The reason we hate one another and fear one another is that we secretly or openly hate and fear our own selves. And we hate ourselves because the depths of our being are a chaos of frustration and spiritual misery. Lonely and helpless, we cannot be at peace with others because we are not at peace with ourselves, and we cannot be at peace with ourselves because we are not at peace with God.[148]

[148] Thomas Merton, *The Living Bread* (London: Burns and Oates, 1976) p.9

The claim of the Christian faith is that when our multiplicity is pointed towards God we find an inner unity and we are at peace. God is the well around which the sheep of our identity can congregate. We think we need to boundary ourselves off and define ourselves around external factors but in fact we are called to have a single mindedness on God who is multiple and yet one; singular in community, alone and together. All voices, desires, identities fade when we intentionally exist within His. This is what it means to be 'in Christ'.

There's a much larger conversation to be had here around the Christian understanding of God in Trinity and how it contrasts with the secular utopian vision of peaceful cohabitation. I am yet to be convinced that a politic that merely wishes and forces peace between differing viewpoints is any kind of peace at all. If 'peace' and understanding is forced, then it is a violence of the most awful kind ("You will get on whether you want to or not!") Society has tried to force unity by building walls around those they want to keep together against their will!

Our understanding of Christian community, a unifying of ontological difference, as an incarnation and embodying of the Triune God, can speak into the social ethics of our current culture. John Milbank, a theologian working in the UK, sees our culture understanding difference as entering, 'the existing common cultural space only to compete, displace or expel... each new difference has a limitless ambition to obliterate all others, and therefore to cancel out difference itself.'[149] Stanley Hauerwas suggests,

> The best that secular peace can hope for then, is a 'tolerable' regulation or management of conflict by one coercive means or another.[150]

Out of fear, we box others in to control and understand them or

---

[149] Milbank, *Theology and Social Theory*, p.290

[150] Hauerwas, *Performing the Faith*, p.87

to give ourselves justification for avoiding others as 'not like me'. We label others so that our outer life makes sense, in the vain hope that, in turn, our inner life will too. We want to tame and subdue the environment around us to make us feel safe and in control whilst the uncontrollable, plural voices in our own selves continue unabated. We're not safe inside so we go outside.

It is a built in, basic component of being human; we care about what our social group think of us; we crave to be part of a family, a pack, a clan. This comes down to survival. We have learnt, over millennia that, isolation and loneliness kills; even the hardwired introverts amongst us need other people in order to live. So, we build walls around those people we care about and box them in to keep them close.

If we lose someone we care about, either through death or broken relationship, there is an intrinsic understanding that we lose a part of us; the more intense and intimate the relationship, the greater the loss. Like two plasters that get stuck together and then ripped apart, pieces that were once of you go with the other. We are continually shaped and molded by the relationships we hold. In order to protect ourselves from losing a hold on our identity we must hold onto those who have helped us to construct them, particularly those who have constructed our deepest parts. We all know through experience, however, that this is an impossible task and loss, bereavement and separation is part of life. People come and go and to build the walls around people, to stop them leaving, all that protection, is futile. We continue to do it because the alternative is scary; to be alone, either in an overwhelming mass where one is not seen, known and acknowledged except as a fraction of the collective or isolated, without others, outside the tribe; vulnerable. We meet again this paradox in human existence; individual selfhood and the need for communality, a family/tribe/social group. We build walls to shut people out or to keep people in. All this construction communicates our conviction for community and, at the same time the sub-conscious, futile act of trying to control our own character.

Our lives are a mess of contradictions, discrepancies and conflict between what we want, what we say and what we do. We forget or want to erase things that don't fit our own view of ourselves whilst we embellish or remember those bits that fit our own self-perception. This view of our self is distorted and skewed, either positively or negatively, by what we hear and experience as response to our actions and words. If we are told that certain behaviour is "disgusting" but we fail to adapt or stop such conduct, then we can begin to see ourselves as "disgusting"; that is who we are to ourselves. Likewise, if we are told that we have a beautiful voice repeatedly then we come to believe that we are a born singer. When we come in contact with another view of us that contradicts this self-belief then we experience conflict. We respond by either rejecting the new view of our self or re-define our own held view.

This contact with opposing views and statements about our selfhood is painful, confusing and is a fundamental challenge to the order of our inner reality. No wonder we resist these moments so strongly. It is this conflict, which breaks relationships. But it is also these moments that hold the great potential of binding us together. We must all, if we are to truly relate, risk vulnerability; the dangerous act of removing walls, around ourselves and around those we allow to shape our lives. Removing the walls, however, brings up the opposite problem; how do we define a community without walls? What is it that makes 'us', 'us', if we are not distinct from 'them'?

In Shinar the focus is this central tower of strength. There is nothing to stop people walking far away, leaving the community behind and going at it alone. What holds this community together is not some outer limit passed which they may never return. There is no line, which, if crossed, they are then deemed 'outside', separates, 'excluded', but they have this central point which draws people in, a focus, a hub; the heart of the community, deep wells. If anyone strays too far away from this, they seem to struggle and begin to weaken; they start to feel less complete.

We as humans already know about the strength at the middle rather than on the outside. It's the difference between an armadillo and a Dime bar[151] that comes down to two forms of skeletons which give shape to many animals in our natural world: endoskeletons and exoskeletons. Exoskeletons, like armadillos, have the bones and structure on the outside giving solid protection to a flexible core whereas endoskeletons, like humans, have a solid core and a flexible, malleable outer layer.

When the Church describes itself as a body this should hint towards where the definition should be and how we should interact on our outer limits. In Shinar they proudly achieved an endoskeletal community, which allowed fluidity and change to occur whilst holding onto a core. This seems to be an excellent model for community which risks vulnerability and is flexible to the changes; the loss, separation from others, etc. that are part of life. As we try and construct healthy, growing, organic society it seems this form allows growth and sustainability, much more than boundaries and walls ever could.

But Shinar did not survive. They built their tower and God came down and disrupted it. Why? God is either a petty, cosmic killjoy or there was something that they couldn't see as they constructed the 'perfect' society and peaceful, harmonious co-habitation. It is true that societies function better when there is a shared vision and purpose, people are drawn to where there is life but, in Shinar, where was the source of that life? Human beings.

We can achieve great things. We are powerful beings made in the image of God, but we are not God. This is where the people of Shinar went wrong. They built a tower around what they can

---

[151] In the 1990's there was an advertising campaign for the chocolate bar, Dime. A farmer is approached by TV presenter and asked to try a Dime bar. The farmer takes a bite and the presenter asks, "Do you like the surprising combination of crisp caramel stuff and delicious milk chocolate; soft on the outside and crunchy of the inside?" "Nope. I like armadillos. Crunchy on the outside and soft in the middle. Armadillos!" The tag line for this chocolate bar was 'a surprising alternative to armadillos.'

achieve, what they can imagine but that can never compare to the perfection and wisdom of God. We can learn all manner of things, we can gather insights and systems, but all will fall short of God's plans and purposes because we can never be gods. We are restricted beings; we came from dust and to dust we shall return. We will always be creatures not Creators. It is only when we humbly draw close to the Creator of the universe and receive new life from him through the waters of baptism that we truly grow. All other things are short-lived and fallible.

If we are not being made holy by being in relationship with God, we are being made unholy. If we are not drawing close to the wells of his Spirit, we are walking away. There is no such thing as standing still in the process of sanctification; we're always moving in one direction or the other. A sacred community is one that is defined, not by an extoskeleton, a cast around a limb, but, rather, an endoskeleton; a form around which we gather. Sanctification, the redefinition of our being, occurs when we are in pure communion with the divine source of holiness and true life.

Obedience

...faith exists only in obedience, is never without obedience. Faith is only faith in deeds of obedience.[152]

> Listen, my son, and with your heart hear the principles of your Master. Readily accept and faithfully follow the advice of a loving Father, so that through the labour of obedience you may return to Him from whom you have withdrawn because of the laziness of disobedience. My words are meant for you whoever you are, who laying aside your own will, take up the all-powerful and righteous arms of obedience to fight under the true King, the Lord Jesus Christ.[153]

Thus starts the Rule of St. Benedict. It begins with an unswerving command to obedience, not a popular command in our individualised, self-autonomous culture but, as we have said, the monastic life centres on the vow to stability, conversion and obedience. Columba Cary-Elwes helpfully highlights that 'the very word obedience has a treasure hidden in its history.' She writes,

> If you unpack it, ob audiere, to listen intently is the language of love. When you really love, you listen intently to know what the one you love wants to happen.[154]

This understanding of obedience is just about acceptable in the context of our personal relationship with Christ but it becomes

---

[152] Bonhoeffer, *Discipleship*, p.64
[153] RB Pro:1-5
[154] Columba Cary-Elwes, *Work and Prayer:the rule of St. Benedict for lay people* (London:Burns & Oates, 1992) p.182

problematic for many in our postmodern, subjective culture when applied to fellow human beings. To love and obey another is seen by our self-autonomous society as oppressive and open to all manner of abuse. This resistance to trust those in authority has also begun to destabilize our society as institutions crumble under the shame of their own hypocrisy and the Emperors' clothes no longer go through the wash! How do we rebuild community in the rubble of so many broken pedestals?

In describing the importance of the abbot in his Rule, St. Benedict quotes Christ, "Whoever listens to you, listens to me."[155] Christ imparts authority to his disciples in order that they may speak on his behalf to others. The abbot in the monastic community is to represent Christ to his monks. The risk of abuse to that kind of power is real and Cary-Elwes acknowledges as much when she states,

> No doubt also an abbot can go beyond his rights, and what is wrong or evil should not be obeyed. Yet all that happens is under divine providence and God's wise guidance of the world, and this includes commands of superiors.[156]

St. Benedict spends many chapters portraying what an abbot should and should not do; he spends so much time that it begs the question, "why is it so important?" It is important because the role of the abbot directly impacts the spiritual formation and discipleship of the rest of the community. 'The first thing that defines the abbot,' Esther de Waal writes, 'is not the position at the head of an institution but his relationship with sons' She links this with the model of discipleship undertaken by monks.

---

[155] RB 5:6,15
[156] Cary-Elwes, *Work and Prayer*, p.40

> The learning process is more analogous to that of apprenticeship by which one person learns a skill from another. In the ancient world skills were handed down from father to son, and so apprenticeship also carries with it the implication of a father-son relationship. It involves imitation and long, patient watching and copying, a shared learning that owes much to the fact of daily living together.[157]

St. Benedict is keen to emphasize the responsibility of leadership within the monastic life as being primarily spiritual; there are management concerns, yes, but this 'leader' 'will be accountable on Judgement Day for his teaching and the obedience of his charges'[158], 'he should know that the greater his trust, the greater the responsibility'[159] and he 'must not undervalue or overlook the salvation of his charges. Thus he must always remember his task is the guidance of souls (for which he will be held accountable) and he must put aside the worldly, transitory and petty things.'[160] In this way my understanding of my priestly and parochial ministry, the 'cure of souls' to which I have made a promise to possess with my bishop, although it makes entering religious orders complicated, enables me to understand the role of authority and the monastic vow of obedience in my life.

Obedience, for St. Benedict, is dependent upon the reality of the familial relationship between two parties and that relationship is established on a shared life of humility under the authority of God which he imparts to His apostles. In the gospels Jesus declares, 'All authority in heaven and on earth has been given to me.' He then continues to commission His followers to go and continue His ministry under that authority. Elsewhere in the gospels Jesus gives His disciples authority to perform certain tasks. Jesus is clearly not

---

[157] de Waal, *Seeking God*, p.130

[158] RB 2:6

[159] RB 2:30

[160] RB 2:33-34

averse to authority and places that authority within human relationships. Authority, however, is abused; that's a fact of life. We can all reel out stories of how someone in authority has abused that position to meet their own needs. No area of life has been immune to this experience and that needs to be said and heard. This does not mean that authority is, in itself, bad or negative. Personally, I have had problems with authority, but I have found it helpful to put a face to those problems and rather than dismiss 'authority' because it hurt me, to name the person in that position who hurt me. It is too easy to blame some faceless vehicle of abuse rather than face the personal perpetrator; to protest against 'the Church', 'the ordained office' or whatever it is rather than name the specific person.

Life without authority, in my experience, is actually just as painful and difficult as life with it. It is in the vacuum of authority that skewed and extremist views emerge and grow. As human beings we hunger and thirst for an authoritative narrative to live within and, when we are starved of it, we'll settle for the closest thing. In the absence of a shared story, western societies have bred polemical, competing ideologies which hold little of the nuance of a worked through framework. We have deconstructed and abandoned the old paths, well-trod by our ancestors, with juvenile passion and boldness.

There is a generalized view that 'millennials', the generation who grew up saddling the millennium, have no respect for authority. In reality I think we do respect authority, but we do not acknowledge them, as an acknowledgement of them would insist that we were not totally independent and 'free'. These more subtle authorities hold sway over their subjects and coerce an unconscious obedience from them. They maintain this power by continuing to challenge the very idea of authority which they freely exert on people in order that any alternative that challenges their influence can be undermined swiftly and easily. This leads to the dangerous tendency to dismiss clear, transparent authority whilst allowing deceptive and sycophantic forms to hold power over us. For millennials the primary authority is no longer placed with the previous generations but rather in peers and this is what has led to the forms of ideologies which many follow with blind obedience as these worldviews connect deeply with the narcissism inherent in the psychology of millennial generation.

"The past has failed us," millennials say, "Let us reconstruct the world afresh."

Blogger, Anna Mussmann, wrote an interesting critique on this culture using the popular fiction that young adults read. The article, provocatively called 'Millennials Think Authority Figures Are Untrustworthy Idiots, And Modern Culture Is To Blame' explores what these books have taught, primarily millennials, as they have developed their worldview. Mussmann argues,

> When young adult fiction encourages reliance on transitory, peer-based relationships, it casts off the unifying role that classic literature once played. Our stories no longer bind multiple generations together. Instead they divide them... we even structure young people's lives in ways that decrease adult influence and increase peer culture: our children are separated by age at school and attend age-specific youth programs at church (often never participating in traditional services that are designed for all-ages). They listen to their own music and text in their own language. The qualities which unify a culture, such as music, etiquette rules, and stories, are all things of which youth have their own.[161]

This article is fascinating when considering a prevailing attitude to obedience in millennials to authority figures of older

---

[161] Anna Mussman, 'Millenials Think Authority Figures Are Untrustworthy Idiots, And Modern Culture Is To Blame', The Federalist, February 4th 2014, http://thefederalist.com/2014/01/23/millennials-think-authority-figures-are-untrustworthy-idiots-and-modern-culture-is-to-blame

generations, but I don't want to dismiss my generation too quickly. There must always be an earning of trust and some blame must fall onto the previous generation who, after dismissing their parents for the mess of two world wars and the violent climax of enlightenment and modernism, felt they should never impose obedience on their children. In this context is it any wonder that the millennial generation today have little to no compass to guide them through the chaotic path of adolescence and adulthood.

The heady mix of my generation with my parents' generation when running a society, is a cocktail for increasingly isolated people with highly subjective opinions to right and wrong trying to co-habit a claustrophobic space which leads inevitably to an increase in violence, physically and politically. Our politic is broken because we have taken a shared narrative away and allowed a vacuum to be created. We now happily worship this 'absence' in true nihilistic fashion.

> Many young adults, especially those from the less affluent backgrounds, feel that they live in a world where family and community have eroded to the point of dysfunction. Personal loyalty may be their only hope in a dark, chaotic, and existential world. This kind of loyalty is the same moral value on which both gangs and tribes are built, and in many ways, our culture encourages a new kind of clique-like tribalism. Paradoxically, however, such loyalty is also constantly mutating, because our peer-oriented relationships (friendships and marriages) are self-chosen and therefore dissolvable. In real life the group loyalties break and reconfigure under strain. Such single-generation tribalism is also incredibly narrow. G. K. Chesterton argues that families are far more broadening than self-chosen companions because they force

> individuals to learn to understand many kinds of people.[162]

The monastic vows of stability, conversion and obedience counteract this dangerous 'clique-like tribalism'. Chesterton's point brings us back to our argument in favour of stability and communal learning that we explored before.

Let's return to Jürgen Moltmann's three paradigm's of the Church and reflect again on his words about the Charismatic paradigm particularly. He wrote 'no one has a higher or lower position than anyone else with what he or she can contribute to the community, all are accepted just as they are.' He went on to say, '...Everyone is an expert in his or her own life and personal calling.'[163] And there it is: the mantra for the Church at the present time. No one can tell anyone what is right or wrong. All must be accepted and placed as equally authoritative and by so doing authority is displaced and no longer shared.

The Church is currently facing a new social rebellion akin to the Great Reformation and again it is about power and authority. The Reformation caused authority to be placed in Scripture and thus power/authority was placed in the hands of any who could read and interpret the text. Richard Hooker, the architect of Anglican ecclesiology, later stated the need for three authorities: Scripture, tradition and reason, with Scripture having a form of primacy.

I believe we have seen an ascendance of reason as the primary authority under which the others must fall but, with the advent of charismatic theology, there is a need to rightly emphasise the Holy Spirit's authority in the Church which has morphed intellectual reason to 'experience'. I would say that the Holy Spirit is in all of these, but I understand the move from reason to experience and it comes down to semantics for me. I would argue, however, that this

---

[162] Ibid.

[163] Ibid., p.23-25

'experience' has been adopted by our individualised culture, abandoning objective truth and making 'reason', subjective experience and this is now our sole authority. It is the individualised experience, by way of the charismatic evangelical tradition being allowed to continue without rigorous ecclesiological or pneumatologically questions being asked, that is now seen in most Church debates. The vast majority of decisions now are made on the basis of individualised experience which is a distorted understanding of reason and from this Scripture is re-interpreted and tradition is changed. If authority is not only innately wanted but is also needed for a society to function, how might we seek a renewal of our current understanding of authority to challenge the current culture?

I would argue that, for a society to function, authority must remain external to the self. Narcissistic tribalism is not a healthy way to exist but there are elements of it that should be encouraged; togetherness, sociality, loyalty but in C.S. Lewis' 'Chronicles of Narnia' this balance between friendship and authority is beautifully portrayed in the character of Aslan. This authority figure manages to remain aloof and commanding over the children as they learn to negotiate the strange and dangerous world of Narnia whilst embodying a familial, stable support in their lives. The form of authority portrayed in Lewis' central character is particularly interesting when seen alongside an ensemble theatre model of leadership.

In ensemble theatre practice the challenge for the director is to balance their dual vocation of 'decision maker' and 'guide'. Peter Brook articulates this tension beautifully.

> Half of directing is, of course, being a director, which means taking charge, making decisions… The other half of directing is maintaining the right direction. Here, the director becomes guide… he has to have studied the maps… He searches all the time, but not haphazardly… a

> man looking for gold may ask a thousand questions, but they all lead back to gold.[164]

This same struggle can be seen in the role of an abbot in St. Benedict's depiction of fatherly leadership.

> The abbot must always remember what he is and be mindful of his calling... He should recognize the difficulty of his position – to care for and guide the spiritual development of many different characters. One must be led by friendliness, another by sharp rebukes, another by persuasion. The abbot must adapt himself to cope with individuality so that no member of the community leaves and he may celebrate the monastery's growth.[165]

Brook goes on to describe the complex interaction around power experienced in the pursuit of more egalitarian model of theatre.

> [The director] does not ask to be God and yet his role implies it. He wants to be fallible, and yet an instinctive conspiracy of the actors is to make him the arbiter, because an arbiter is so desperately wanted all the time.[166]

This instinctive arbitration takes us back to Stanley Hauerwas' representation of liberal democracy explored in the context of the vow to stability. He proposed that a society which makes 'freedom an end in itself' must become 'excessively legalistic.'[167] At the heart of the liberal political theory is the idea that 'a people do not need a shared story; all they need is a system of rules that will

---

[164] Peter Brook, *The Shifting Point: 40 years of theatrical exploration 1946-1987* (London: Methuen, 1989) p.5-6
[165] RB 2:30-32
[166] Brook, *The Empty Space*, p. 43
[167] Hauerwas, *Community of Character*, p.75

constitute procedures for resolving disputes as they pursue their various interests.'[168] In this environment the 'guide' is transformed from fellow traveler to authoritative arbiter and the role of leader loses the creative tension which defends it from becoming overly dictatorial.

Hauerwas also argues that 'the ethical and political theory necessary to such a form of society [is] that the individual is the sole source of authority.' It is in this presentation that we see the root of the obvious conflict in a political theory that states the individual is the sole source of authority whilst simultaneously imposing an authoritative, legalistic framework in order to sustain such autonomy. So, if authority is removed from the individual to remove the need for arbitration and is not placed in a society's legalistic framework, where should it be found?

The model of leadership sought for in ensemble theatre practice and articulated in the Rule of St. Benedict asserts an authority agreed upon by the community and maintained by the role of the director/abbot who becomes a kind of 'story-keeper'. This role ensures that authority is clearly named and placed in the reality of the community's shared life. Hauerwas concludes,

> [the Church's] first social task in any society is to be herself... to be the kind of community that recognizes the necessity that all societies... require authority... [and] our authority is neither in society itself nor in the individual; it is in God.[169]

The challenge remains for the individual who inhabits the role of leader to continually remain mindful of the 'instinctive conspiracy' of the other members of a group to make the leader into an arbiter as they subtly relinquish responsibility for communal obedience to the greater authority. They must constantly avoid the

[168] Ibid., p.78
[169] Ibid., p.83-84

temptation to become overly paternalistic in enforcing a form of heteronomy. If the leader fails in this task they slip into more abusive forms of authority and do great harm to the appreciation of authority itself. The selection of such a person must be made on the basis of their proven record of living as one under authority themselves; they must invite obedience as they have inhabited it themselves.

The role of ensemble theatre director/abbot only makes sense within the wider context of the community in which it is placed. It requires an explicit articulation of the limits of its power; the leader must remain under authority themselves. Obedience should never only be found under the leader but equally found within that role too. A director, within the ensemble theatre practice, must be under the authority of the company to enable them to faithfully articulate their shared narrative in performance. Joan Littlewood, Artistic Director of Theatre Workshop and a major promoter of ensemble theatre practice in the UK, powerfully said in a radio interview,

> I think the worship of the genius producer is deadly… we are in the age of community. My belief is in the genius of each person and this form of collaboration can reveal something unique, which is more important than any one producer superimposing on a cast.[170]

Littlewood embodied a 'socialist political conviction that stressed the value and importance of the group over and above the individual.'[171] Both Brook and Littlewood's style of directing can be seen as an outworking of Joseph Myers' concept of 'organic order'. In his book 'Organic Community', Myers shows how a 'master plan' approach to church growth and community creation is not only common but also an imitation of a capitalist framework to

---

[170] Joan Littlewood in a radio interview, cited in Nadine Holdsworth, *Joan Littlewood* (Oxon: Routledge, 2006) p.48
[171] Ibid., p.49

organizing living organisms. He suggests churches adoption of 'vision statements' can be perceived as 'master plans'. 'Master plans', Myers says, 'intend to control the future… [and] do not allow for flexibility, uncertainty or serendipity – ingredients of the 'aha' moment.'[172]

> Leaders put their faith in master plans because they have greater faith in master plans than they do in people. Plans are more predictable and easier to control than people. And who controls the plan? Usually one person.[173]

It is within this capitalist context that leaders have begun to be more obedient to plans, initiatives and strategies than to people. It is after this shift that we begin to experience the degradation and humiliation that comes with abuse of power. We become pawns in a game rather than treasured companions in a journey. St. Benedict wants the abbot to model his leadership on Christ who, as we saw in our chapter on redemption, was 'self-determined and self-limited'[174]

Dietrich Bonhoeffer, discussing community, suggests,

> Innumerable times a whole Christian community has broken down because it had sprung from a wish dream… God hates visionary dreaming… Christian brotherhood is not an ideal which we must realize; it is a reality created by God in Christ in which we may participate.[175]

It is the leader's task, in this ensemble model, to relinquish their own individual, visionary dreams and risk being susceptible to the gifts of others by actively participating in the wider story of the community. In the case of an abbot they must learn to receive the

---

[172] Myers, *Organic Community*, p.28
[173] Ibid., p.67
[174] Gorringe, *God's Theatre*, p.12
[175] Dietrich Bonhoeffer, *Life Together* (London: SCM Press, 1954) p.15-16

community as a gift and tenderly enable them to faithfully articulate their shared life in performance. Obedience can become a reality when there is a trusting, familial relationship between the one who offers it and the one who obediently receive it as gift. A leader must become obedient to the community just as much as the community becomes obedient to them; obedience, therefore, must become mutual within the context of trusting, familial relationships. But obedience is not easy and must be undertaken as a discipline.

'Being disciplined in obedience' Stanley Hauerwas argues, 'is perhaps the key virtue of a good and faithful performer. This is a skill that can be acquired only in communities that foster an "ecology of hope," what Nicholas Lash calls "schools of stillness, of attentiveness; of courtesy, respect and reverence' academies of contemplativity."'[176] Hauerwas' exploration of improvisation as a model for understanding Christian discipleship continues to marry the ensemble theatre practice with intentional Christian communities.

> ...the patience of a good performer requires a doing but also and equally important a suffering, an undergoing, a giving up, a receptivity, a capitulation. This giving up, however, is more a giving over or dispossession of oneself... This ability to let go of oneself, to dispossess oneself in the very execution of the act, is a skill that is not learned quickly or easily and certainly not on one's own. Indeed, if acquired at all, it is learned in communion and fellowship with others over the course of an entire Christian life.[177]

This beautifully brings the vows of stability and obedience together as we begin to see, not only the necessity of trust and

---

[176] Hauerwas, *Performing the Faith*, p.100
[177] Ibid., p.100-101

faithfulness to one another but also how we might extend or deepen that trust in community. Obedience, within the environment of a stable community, stops being an arbitrary following of rules and commands from above but a mutual sharing of a way of life walked together under theonomy.

It is key, therefore, that an abbot inhabits the role, divested to him by God's authority, with the humility it demands. One abbot who articulated this humility well was St Aelred of Rievaulx,

> To you, my Jesus, I confess, therefore; to you, my Saviour and my hope, to you, my comfort and my God, I humbly own that I am not as contrite and as fearful as I ought to be for my past sins; nor do I feel enough concern about my present ones. And you, sweet Lord, have set a man like this over your family, over the sheep of your pasture. Me, who take all too little trouble with myself, you bid to be concerned on their behalf; and me, who never pray enough about my own sins, you would have pray for them. I, who have taught myself so little too, have also to teach them. Wretch that I am, what have I done? What have I undertaken? What was I thinking of? Or rather, sweetest Lord, what were you thinking of regarding this poor wretch?[178]

As we read St. Benedict's 'qualities' of an abbot the expectations placed upon one person are overwhelming; the wisdom required, impossible, unless you were the second incarnation of Christ Himself. It is easy to read St. Benedict's depiction, in our current culture, fascinated with 'the leader', as a job description. St. Benedict begins, however by stating, 'Always remember, concerning the election of an abbot, that he should be

[178] St Aelred of Rievaulx, *Treatises and Pastoral Prayer* (Michigan: Cistercian Publications, 1995) p.107-108

chosen by the entire community.'[179] A leader is, before God, just another monk, dearly loved but desiring no individuality. As St. Benedict says, '…let everyone stay in his own place for "whether bond or free we are all one in Christ" (Gal 3:28; Eph 6:8) and are equal in the service of the Lord; with God there is no respecter of individuals.'[180]

An abbot should not desire the role of authority for himself and should, along with the other monks, take responsibility for his own faithfulness and obedience under God. From this place, the call to discipline and rebuke is tempered with grace and humility. As an abbot is called forth by the community then the community commit to praying and supporting him. Even if they don't see him as 'Christ's representative' they are called to encourage him to be transformed into His likeness. No abbot is perfect because no human is. The qualities outlined in this chapter of St. Benedict's Rule are not to be achieved prior to appointment but are rather the pattern that God will now shape them into. The abbot, after appointment, now looks to allowing God to shape him in this particular way.

I want to finish this exploration of the particular roles of authority by discussing the relationship between role and gifting, and to do so in that order. This relationship is commonly spoken of in these terms: one receives spiritual gifts, given by grace to all, and then, after receiving, one discovers the call to a particular ministry within God's mission. I see, however, through Scripture, men and women being called first and equipped second; Abraham and Sarah, Moses, Samuel, David, Mary, Peter, Matthew… It is only in this order can we take on roles of responsibility with the humility characterized by St. Aelred of Rievaulx.

All calls from God should call from us humble confusion as to how we could possibly do what He is asking of us. If we, when we

---

[179] RB 64:1

[180] RB 2:19-20

hear His call into a particular ministry/task say "Oh, that makes sense because you've given me these gifts to do it." Then there's no humility; you are trusting the gift before the giver. The concern I have with the pattern of discussion around spiritual gifts and ministry is that if the gifts are given before any task is commanded by God, then you limit what God will ask of you. This is particularly instilled when we are given only one spiritual gift. If we begin by asking "Lord, what is it you want me to do, poor as I am?" then God can call you anywhere to do anything. It is right and Scriptural to respond, "How am I to do that, poor as I am?" And He will respond, "I will give to you what you need; the words, the strength, the insight. Follow my Spirit and all things will be made available." Once the task is done, we turn and ask again, "What now?" He can still, if He is able to give more gifts for new tasks, command you to go somewhere else, where you have no experience and no skills. "That's foolishness!" you say, "Why doesn't He keep me on my career ladder building on from where I ended?" Because, it's not about what you can do but what He can do. He wants to show His glory and power because there is no other way you could achieve things He wants to achieve through you.

The role of the other monks, therefore, is to receive the abbot's ministry as from God. To pray that God will use the abbot for the spiritual growth of His Kingdom. The abbot will not always do so as obediently as the monks or God would have liked but they forgive and encourage to see God use the broken vessel for His glory and His Kingdom.

Brian C Taylor suggests that 'any choice brings with it limits and rules to which we must be obedient in order to be fulfilled.'[181] which echoes what we've already discussed about our current relationship with choice. We interpret our 'freedom of choice' as meaning that we are free to choose. We are in one way, free to choose but in another we rarely make a choice as we rarely

[181] Taylor, Spirituality for Everyday Living, p.26

embrace the obedience required to fulfill that choice. Remember the example of the trainers? In choosing one pair of trainers we are setting limits in that we are saying it is those trainers and not any other. If we are to be obedient to that choice, we must deny the consumerist culture's demands to choose the upgrade or to 'shop around'. Perpetual choice keeps the consumerist culture going and, in order to escape it, we must be well practiced in the art of obedience.

A similar example can be made in the context of identity. At the heart of our culture is the glorification of the freedom to be ourselves, autonomy, to find out our own way. This parenting and educational approach stems from the seeming failure of previous generations in the emergence of two world wars, the horrors of the Holocaust and other genocides and the creation of the atomic bomb. The previous generations have become paralyzed morally and delegate authority onto the individuality of their children. Brian C Taylor continues,

> The freedom to find out for ourselves what works and what doesn't is no freedom at all but rather an imprisonment to the limits of our own imagination and intelligence.[182]

In this lack of authority when it comes to raising children and young people ironically imprisons them to repeat the past with no sense of history and tradition that, on the whole, protected previous ages. Cross-generational relationship have been eroded as older people are unable to train and disciple younger members of communities in the shared narrative as there remains little to no desire to share that story and by teaching the young requires them to allow their perceived 'freedom' to be denied. To reopen a conversation on the nature of obedience, I believe, will begin the healing of society as we reclaim the way of teaching and instructing

---

[182] ibid., p.27

one another, learning from the past and growing together. Dominic Milroy, in his paper "Education According to The Rule of St. Benedict" articulates this well when he wrote,

> Obedience is not an imposed subservience to an external authority but a condition of inward growth... All disobedience represents, in this sense, the pursuit of an illusory freedom which obstructs the acquisition of real freedom.'[183]

As we explored in the chapter on study, there is a counter-intuitive truth that real freedom is found within the bounds of obedience. The New Monastic Movement must begin to model and live out lives of obedience, not just to God but to one another too. We must explicitly challenge both heteronomous and autonomous understandings of authority and fully embrace and live out the theonomous life of a communal Rule. Stanley Hauerwas, again,

> ...it is the Christian belief that true freedom comes by learning to be appropriately dependent, that is, to trust the one who wills to have us as his own and who wills the final good of all. In more traditional language, for the Christian to be perfectly free means to be perfectly obedient. True freedom is perfect service.[184]

To engage in community is to learn to deny one's self and serve the other. In this obedience and commitment, we learn a real freedom; the gift from God who gave it to the one who was obedient, even to death on a cross. We too can partake in that same freedom if we follow in the footsteps of Jesus who walks the path ahead of us. In order to experience it though will require we obey His call and He has chosen to place all His followers into His

---

[183] Dominic Milroy, "Education According to The Rule of St. Benedict", Ampleforth Journal, no.84 (Autumn 1979) p.4
[184] Hauerwas, *A Community of Character*, p.131

Body, the Church. It is in engaging in the life of imperfect human beings that we learn how to live like Christ who came and embraced our broken humanity in order to redeem it for His glory.

The final word is to be given to Philip Lawrence, abbot of the Monastery of Christ in the Desert who proposes,

> There is a real formation in having to deal with other human persons in a community and with having to learn to live with a superior who is not perfect and yet to whom we give our obedience.[185]

[185] Philip Lawrence, "Chapter 1: the kinds of monks", The Monatery of Christ in the Desert, https://christdesert.org/prayer/rule-of-st-benedict/chapter-1-the-kinds-of-monks/

Service

"O God, who art the author of peace and lover of concord, in knowledge of whom standeth our eternal life, whose service is perfect freedom."[186]

We have explored, throughout this book, the nature of freedom. The freedom promised by our culture is no freedom at all but an enslavement to a life of perpetual searching with no destination. In the eternal wilderness of solitary existence, there is no home, there is no peace, and all are free to wander further from the community we are built for. The Church needs to recapture a vison for a shared life, bound together by a shared narrative, shared principles and shared practices. These will define us; or rather, they will re-define us but not externally like the Law or a wall but internally like a well of the Spirit. By this we are 'sanctified by the Spirit' (1 Pet 1:2) and set apart from the dust and made into living creatures.

We discover, as we draw near to God, we also draw near to those who also draw near to Him. We find ourselves gathered around the same well, drinking the same water and being nourished by the same source. Our commitment to God, therefore, is reliant, in part, upon our commitment to others. We find that we are bound to each other because we are bound to God. D.T. Niles, a 20th century Ceylonese pastor, once wrote, 'Christianity is one beggar telling another beggar where he found bread.'[187] and this requires that we listen, in obedience, to His Spirit speaking through His Church, as we lead one another to the source of life.

Evagrius' threefold formation culminates in *theoria theologike* the contemplation of the Holy Trinity. This stage is depicted as an indwelling of God within a person in pure

---

[186] Book of Common Prayer, Collect for Peace

[187] D.T. Niles, *The New York Times*, May 11, 1986, Section 6, p.38

communion. Hugh of St Victor's system of study, likewise, focused on the building, by God, of a dwelling place for Himself in the life of a disciple. It concludes with the dwelling being 'decorated by the laying on of color.'[188] Hugh describes this as a virtuous life, one of embodied moral action. The process would not have been deemed 'successful', to Hugh, if the student did not live out, in action, their reformed life. Hugh of St Victor's work is part of a reformation period in monastic theology as they attempted to recapture the rightful balance between contemplation and action. Prior to the Canon regulars (of which Hugh was a member) and the mendicant orders, monastics generally considered, 'contemplation as pure pleasure, and action as pure affliction.'[189] Hugh and others contributed to the restored relationship between contemplation and action and we have been able to articulate the discovery that 'action is the spring and contemplation the source.'[190] The result of contemplation is pure communion with the Divine source and an indwelling of God Himself by His Holy Spirit. As He makes his dwelling within us, we are caught up in His Divine movement. We find ourselves inspired to act as we are called to participate in His work of restoration, reconciliation and redemption. These inspired actions are what we will define as 'service'; all Divine works that we participate in.

In the face of continuous reports of declining numbers of people ascribing to Christianity, the Church has set itself to 'mission mode'. The issue with this rise in missiological conversations as a reaction to dwindling attendance in church services is that the emphasis of mission can be unhelpfully biased towards numerical growth. Mission, in this context, can too easily fit into a narrative of transferring 'them' to 'us'. The pressure of

---

[188] Didascalicon 6.2

[189] Hans Urs von Balthasar, Exploration in Theology, vol. 1: the word made flesh (San Francisco: Ignatius Press, 1989) p.231

[190] Thomas Merton, No Man Is An Island (Boston: Shambhala, 2005) p.73

maintaining a particular paradigm of Church causes us to ask deep questions about definition and we immediately look to external boundaries. Mission, outreach, evangelism can all become too consumerist and commercial as we attempt to entice new members to perpetuate our particular vision and master plan. This form of mission, however, relies too much on past 'success' and coercive power. What of humility? What of the commitment to ongoing conversion and learning? What of the vulnerability and openness to gift?

It is right to seek to participate in the 'missio dei', 'the sending of God'. Mission is all about allowing God to send us, by His Spirit, to action His will. When we participate in God's mission we are continuing Christ's work as He obediently incarnated God's will. Our sanctification is manifested in the *way* we perform the work of God not just the performance of God's work. As God dwells within us, our wills are married to God's and we become a new form of incarnation. Our mission should, therefore, be the same character of Christ's, depicted, most beautifully, in Philippians 2:1-18 a life of loving service.

> Missionaries leave the securities of their own culture and make their home among those they are called to share the Gospel with. They pitch their tents in communities in which they are strangers. English Anglicans need to re-discover this heritage and see the 'strange' areas of the country, the 'Bethlehems' and 'Galilees', as primary areas for mission. In so doing the temptation to look to 'successful' congregations and assume that their way can be replicated and franchised out should be avoided since this approach is neither incarnational nor contextually sensitive.[191]

---

[191] Thomson, *Sharing Friendship*, p.163

We need to re-discover contextual evangelism and witness, one birthed from the journey which began 'remember you are dust and to dust you shall return. Turn away from sin and be faithful to Christ'[192] accepting the words, 'You have been clothed with Christ. As many as are baptized into Christ have put on Christ'[193] and travels into the liturgical truth 'God has called you by name and made you his own. Confirm, O Lord, your servant with your Holy Spirit.' God has called us and made us His dwelling place. The word 'confirm' carries connotations of 'holding together' along with a 'strengthening'. Our beings are established and strengthened in this process of sanctification. As God does this we are transformed, we are distinguished. This living out of discipleship in a community distinct by its core will draw others towards the Church.

At the start of our journey together we read Vincent Donovan, a missionary to the Masai people, describe this incarnational witness and 'unpredictable process of evangelization' as

> … a process leading to that new place where none of us has ever been before. When the gospel reaches a people where they are, their response to that gospel is the church in a new place, and the song they will sing is that new, unsung song, that unwritten melody that haunts all of us. What we have to be involved in is not the revival of the church or the reform of the church. It has to be nothing less than what Paul and the Fathers of the Council of Jerusalem were involved in for their time – the refounding of the Catholic church for our age.[194]

We are called to witness to God's transformation of our life. We are called to live in the world as changed people; a people who

[192] The Archbishops' Council, *Times and Seasons*, p.230
[193] The Archbishops' Council, *Christian Initiation*, p. 71
[194] Donovan, *Christianity Rediscovered*, p.xix

are filled with God's Holy Spirit and who are identified with him. Our issue is, out of fear of being despised, we have returned to the security of the ways of the world and have forgotten the counter-cultural narrative that is to shape us. We relativized the life of faith. We have not been hated by the world because we have not demanded from them a response. We lived an indistinct life and told ourselves we were radical.

> Is the price we are paying today with the collapse of the organised church anything else but an inevitable consequence of grace acquired too cheaply? We gave away preaching and sacraments cheaply; we performed baptisms and confirmations; we absolved an entire people, unquestioned and unconditionally; out of human love we handed over what was holy to the scornful and unbelievers. We poured out rivers of grace without end, but the call to rigorously follow Christ was seldom heard.[195]

Being sent somewhere to tell our story is easy. Being sent to live a life dependent on God, to be stripped of all our identities, comfort, power and influence; that's mission. We are looking not to interrupt our lives with acts of service but to find that our life with God is a perpetual life of servanthood to God, with God and by God.

> Service is not a list of things that we do, though in it we discover things to do… To do specific acts of service is not the same thing as living in the discipline of service… it is one thing to act like a servant, it is quite another to be a servant.[196]

---

[195] Bonhoeffer, *Cost of Discipleship*, p.53-54
[196] Foster, *Celebration of Discipline*, p. 165

What we are being called to do is not colonize but to incarnate. Our diplomatic mission is to commit to a strange and foreign world and serve in love; to live a distinct life, allowing God to flow through us with his Holy Spirit. We are, as His Church, called to be a visible, prophetic sign, to witness to the transformation that is possible when you open your life to God. John Thomson powerfully describes it this way: 'The church is the crater left behind by the explosion of God's salvation in Christ.'[197]

The modus operandi of God's restoration plan is generous hospitality towards humanity. Hospitality, in the New Testament, is the translation of a Greek word 'philoxenos', which literally means: "love the stranger". The Latin word means the same thing: 'to entertain strangers'. We were once estranged from God in sin, but, due to His hospitality, we have been welcomed into His family. In His grace He wooed us into friendship and adopted us.

The command to give hospitality to strangers is repeated through the letters of the Early Church. In the New Testament we read it in Hebrews 13:2, Romans 12:13, 1 Peter 4:8-9 and bishops are expected to exemplify this life of hospitality in both 1 Timothy 3:2 and Titus 1:8. The call to seek out the stranger is to train us that love is not about pleasure, or the satisfaction of ourselves but rather is about being in communion with that which is different from us. Covenants and commitments to others should not be about sentiment and enjoyment, for that is a form of self-love, making others into our image rather than encouraging each other to 'be made into a 'likeness' by the exercise of goodness.'[198]

> Indeed, unlike pagan ethic which sought, and in various ways today still seeks, to advocate an ideal of heroic and powerful self-contained agents who can shape the world in their image. Christians seek to be saints whose lives

---

[197] Thomson, *Sharing Friendship*, p.38
[198] Williams, *Wound of Knowledge*, p.28

> witness to what God can do particularly in human weakness.[199]

Our relationships with strangers should seek to embrace difference as God has sought to embrace us and, in indwelling us, transformed us into His likeness: unity in difference.

This is where Anglicanism shines. We are called to live amongst those we share no common interest, political allegiance, philosophical ideology, language or culture. We are called to witness to those we may not share the same language or lifestyle and so we embrace intensely this seeking out of the stranger in order that we may practice real love. This seeking out of the stranger is at the heart of the mission of Christ as He came to seek out sinners, ie. those who are estranged from God.

In Mark 2:13-17 we see just one example of this with Levi/Matthew. Jesus sits and eats with him and his friends and when asked why Jesus answers, "Those who are well have no need of a physician, but those who are sick; I have come to call not the righteous but sinners." I find it ironic that it has become a common defense for some Christians to perceived judgement towards 'sinners' by others to remind the other that Jesus 'hung out with sinners and so should we'. The implication behind this is that the 'judgmental' Christian has failed to love the 'sinner' whilst the 'righteous' Christian will welcome 'sinners' and not judge them. Although it is true to say that Jesus hung out with sinners, it is rarely acknowledged why He did so. Jesus went to 'the sick' because they wanted to be made well and He wanted to 'save' them. He met them in their acknowledgement of sin and their need to change. Indeed, His comment to the Pharisees was a pointed remark as to why they were not asking to be changed. In their chapter on the Church in 'Red Letter Christianity', Shane Claiborne and Tony Campolo quickly begin talking about hypocrisy,

---

[199] Thomson, *Sharing Friendship*, p. 41

> [SHANE:] Here's what I've come to realize: people do not expect Christians to be perfect, but they do expect us to be honest. The problem is that much of the time, we have not been honest. We've pretended to be perfect and pointed fingers at other people.
>
> [TONY:] While Saint Francis recognized the church's failures and hypocrisies, he still saw it as a community of faith where Christ could be encountered. When young people say to me, "I can't be a part of the church because the church is full of hypocrites," I always say, "That's why you are going to feel right at home among us."... In the end, we're all hypocrites.[200]

I'm always struck by the issue Jesus tackled lots: hypocrisy. He does not condemn the Pharisees. He never sought to destroy them or eliminate them; he always sought to name the issue. The Pharisees were not un-saveable, beyond redemption; they were sick like everyone else and Jesus named their sickness; hypocrisy. They wore masks. Jesus loved and respected them and wanted to see the Pharisees healed and flourish. Jesus says that many of the Pharisees are close to the Kingdom of God (Mk 12:28-34).

Our meeting with sinners is to seek to see their healing and transformation from sin but it is also about seeking the continuation of our own conversion and healing. Instead of seeing it as 'us' sitting with 'them' we need to radically see 'us' walking with our fellow sinners closer to the presence of Jesus who wants to heal us *all* of our sin. He will only serve those who want to be served. For we are all dust. We are nothing without him. We all need God's healing and transformation without exception and so Jesus' statement highlights the inner pride of the Pharisees who think they are 'righteous' and basically good. St Paul writes, 'all fall short of

---

[200] Shane Claiborne and Tony Campolo, Red Letter Christianity: living the words of Jesus no matter what' (London: Hodder & Stoughton, 2012), p.

the glory of God' (Rom 3:23) and the irony of the 'righteous' insinuation between Christians on who we treat as 'sinners' is that we betray our own hypocrisy and self-righteousness.

To offer hospitality is to be aware that we are seeking the healing of all creation. We offer hospitality to help us in our own healing of division, prejudice and inner rejection of the other. We offer hospitality to others so we can all experience God's healing welcome into His family. Hospitality is mainly made up of the word 'hospital': a place of refuge and healing. Abigail Van Buren once described the Church by saying that it 'is not a museum for saints - it is a hospital for sinners."[201] We are not the doctor or host. When we consider ourselves in the position of host we are likely to adopt a power over the 'patient'/guest. We are to welcome as Christ welcomed his disciples around His table, on His knees, washing their feet. Christ remains the host and we serve at His table. We are to give honour to the guest as we would to Christ.

> Remember that you were at that time without Christ, being aliens from the commonwealth of Israel, and strangers to the covenants of promise, having no hope and without God in the world. But now in Christ Jesus you who once were far off have been brought near by the blood of Christ. (Eph 2:12-13)

We are fellow guests/patients who are receiving the healing of God through His welcome and hospitality. We are to serve one another and serve those who come to the refuge of God's presence. Within the exchange of gift, blessing and honour between the persons of the Trinity we see a necessity of mutuality as one gives to the other so the other returns. There is a dynamic interplay, particularly articulated in St John's account, between Father, Son

[201] Abigail Van Buren, "Dear Abby: Sinners and Saints!", Park City Daily News, Wednesday 1st April 1964, p.5

and Spirit which we should seek to participate in as recipients of their freely given gift to us.

Our modern, Western world has developed an odd ideal surrounding the notion of gift giving by making the purest gift as unreciprocated. The ideal gift given is one with 'no strings attached'. It is worth noting, along with John Barclay[202], that this is a rare sociological idea and not one shard by St Paul. In the New Testament the language of gift is always reciprocal including the gift of Christ to the world. It would be incongruent to the ancient world to talk of grace as 'unconditional', i.e. requiring no response. The gift of Christ is 'unconditioned' (not requiring any preconditions to receipt of the gift) but it is not 'unconditional'. Gift-giving, for St Paul, is relationship building; it creates social ties. With this understanding, God's gift to us is aimed to build relationship and requires, for the social ties between creature and Creator to be established, a response. Although God gives a gift to all regardless of status and social value, He does give with an expectation that it is reciprocated in some way.

> ...the incongruous and unconditioned gift in Christ is not also unconditional, in the sense of expecting no alteration in the recipient of the gift. God's grace is designed to produce obedience, lives that perform, by heart-inscription, the intent of the Law.[203]

In his discussions on the spiritual gifts in 1 Corinthians 12, St Paul highlights the source of all Divine and spiritual gifts is the Holy Spirit. It is from God who gives us gifts, not because of anything we have done or anything we are but out of His freedom. In the giving of these gifts, however, there is an implicit

---

[202] See John Barclay, *Paul and the Gift* (Grand Rapids: William B Eerdmans Publishing Company, 2015) p.61-65

[203] Ibid., p.492

expectation of how we are to use them. They are not given without expectation. We often forget this within our conversations about ministry and service because we think the discussion is solely about the gifts.

> Now there are a varieties of gifts, but the same Spirit; and there are varieties of services, but the same Lord; and there are varieties of activities, but it is the same God who activates all of them in everyone. To each is given the manifestation of the Spirit for the common good... All these are activated by one and the same Spirit, who allots to each one individually just as the Spirit chooses. (1 Cor 12:4-7, 11)

The Holy Spirit activates in us gifts, services and activities for the 'common good'. The gifts cannot be separated from the service or activity we are to use them for. The gifts are given to enable the service and activity to which we have been called to happen. To possess a gift without performing a service/activity is as impossible as performing a service/activity without the spiritual gifts to activate them. The divorcing of gifts with service/activity often leads us to seeing the gifts as identities; we can easily claim we possess a gift even when we're not utilizing it as though it were tied up in our being. We become boastful of the gift and use it to give us status and power rather than to accept the gift as something to release and use for the common good. They are possessions of the Body of Christ, of which we are individual members.

There is a significant challenge in the Rule of St Benedict and his guidance to craftsman and artisans, '...if anyone becomes proud of his skill and the profit he brings the community, he should be taken from his craft and work at ordinary labor.'[204] God's gifts to us, instead of building social ties and being used for the common good, so often are discussed as divisions of labour amongst the

[204] RB 57:2

Church. As we have already discussed, identifying God's gifts like a spiritual skills audit drastically changes how we understand God's call on our lives. Our interpretation of St Paul's description of the spiritual gifts, however, in light of the expectations of a life of obedient service, allows us to see the full measure of God's abundant and gracious generosity to us.

We claim spiritual giftedness and use it to gain status within the body of Christ as a way to establish our self-esteem because we all are confused about who we are at the deepest level. Thomas Merton, in his extended commentary on identity in 'New Seeds of Contemplation' he says, 'In great saints you find that perfect humility and perfect integrity coincide.'[205] And humility, he asserts, '…consists in being precisely the person you actually are before God, and since no two people are alike, if you have the humility to be yourself you will not be like anyone else in the whole universe.'[206]

For Merton the practical things of everyday life should not be items of conflict,

> The saints do not get excited about the things that people eat and drink, wear on their bodies, or hang on the walls of their houses. To make conformity or non conformity with others in these accidents a matter of life and death is to fill your interior life with confusion and noise.[207]

My personality and my preferences are 'accidents' not to be seen as static like some perfect idol but rather to be sacrificed before God to be used and changed as he wills. My skills and competences, likewise. We must begin to unpick natural and learnt skills/talents from spiritual gifts so as to ensure God's power and grace are revealed more in our lives. This is not to say we should

---

[205] Thomas Merton, New Seeds of Contemplation (New York: New Directions, 1972) p.99

[206] Ibid.

[207] Ibid.

not use these genetic inclinations or practiced expertise for the glory of God but we should not confuse them with the Holy Spirit activated gifts that will equip us for the life of service we are sent, by God, to live.

> Genes, parenting, and spiritual forces do condition who we are. But for believers whose spirits have been regenerated by the Holy Spirit these conditioning factors cannot determine who we are unless we choose to allow them to do so.[208]

On the night that He was betrayed Jesus got up from the table and knelt before His disciples and washed their feet. When He got to Peter, Peter refused, saying, "No. You shall not wash my feet." Jesus demanded that Peter is served. If Peter refuses the gift of service, then Jesus cannot fully give the gift. We can easily do the same with those we serve. We place ourselves within a privileged position of being generous and refusing the person we serve the opportunity to do likewise. There is an implicit power-play which has no place within a sacred community.

We give our gift, given to us by God, to the community for the building up of the Body and for the common good. We give as an act of kenosis as we imitate Christ in His service to us. We give our gift and others receive it with joy, just as we are to look to receive the gift of others with joy. The Church is to be a place of reciprocity of gift as we continually give away the gift God gives. The miraculous multiplying of gift, however, is evident in that, as we give a gift away, we receive fresh gifts.

In this dynamic exchange of gift and service, status is removed. Status, but not authority. Authority becomes a shared possession as all are obedient to one another with some being called, for a time, to serve the community in truly servant hearted

---

[208] Gregory Boyd, *God of the Possible: a biblical introduction to the open view of God* (Grand Rapids: Baker Books, 2000) p.147

leadership and oversight. Others are called to serve the world as God uses them in ministries of reconciliation, encouragement, teaching, guiding, etc. All these activities and service are done by the same Spirit who indwells in us and equips us.

If a community is not engaged in this mission then their discipleship is faulty; just as action is the stream from the source of contemplation, so is mission the fruit of the tree of discipleship. There is no point in just forcing a community to 'do mission' and expect it to work. It would be better to go back to the basics of discipleship; correcting that and the fruit of mission will grow. You judge discipleship by the mission. As Mike Breen argued, 'If you make disciples, you will always get the Church. But if you try to build the Church, you will rarely get disciples.'[209]

And this is why, the Church needs a new form of monasticism; to be a lived expression and model for discipleship in action.

[209] Mike Breen, "Why The Missional Movement Will Fail", Verge Network, http://www.vergenetwork.org/2011/09/14/mike-breen-why-themissional-movement-will-fail/

Conclusion

…It will end with us.

I have tried to argue that the themes encountered on the liturgical journey from Ash Wednesday to Pentecost construct a systematic theology which attempts to paint an a-contextual background for a unifying story. From this background I have drawn out issues that still affect the Church and this has led us to reflect on the emerging movement known as 'New Monasticism'. This journey, however, does not just conclude at the giving of the Holy Spirit but begins a new liturgical season, known as Trinity. It is here where we begin a new adventure together. The landscape is ready for discovery, but it is only as one people, with one story that we will be able to navigate and discern the way forward.

The theology that has been outlined in these pages has naturally taken a Trinitarian shape, not only in the three triptychs of 'Creation, Redemption, Sanctification', 'Stability, Conversion, Obedience' and 'Prayer, Study, Service' but also in the interactions between them all. We have seen that each section has emphasized one person of the Trinity, starting with the Father and concluding with the Spirit but it is not as straight forward as that. For in the beginning the Spirit was at work through Christ, for whom Creation was made. At Christ's birth, death and resurrection, the Spirit was active at the will of the Father and the Spirit's equipping is at the Father's call through the Son. We should not fall into the heretical trap of assuming a form of modalism in the functions of God as Creator, Redeemer and Sanctifier. Rather we should seek to find the beautiful interplay between the three persons in the united work of our one, triune God.

As we set out on our journey together, I acknowledged that the order in which we could explore the three monastic virtues/vows and the three practices could be done in any order and I hope that you have seen that is very much the case. We needed to select one route through these topics and, I feel, that the pathway chosen takes us through the most fruitful reflections. Beginning our interaction with our Creator God with an emphasis on the necessity of humility led us to acknowledge our need to return to our unmasked beginnings by 'staying put' in prayer. We then reflected on the need for a personal conversion and the embrace of transformation achieved, in part, by intentional study and reflections of our Redeemer God. We concluded by exploring our need to accept a life of obedience to our Sanctifying God and, in so doing, obedience to one another in a community committed to service.

When I began writing this book our explorations on obedience was placed alongside the narrative of our redemption and exploration of the practice of study. We could have explored, in great depth the model of obedience seen in the person of Christ and what it meant for Him to be obedient even to death on the cross. To study and learn in community requires obedience, the deep listening to others and that form of listening brings about the necessary change within us.

In the original shape of the book, a commitment to conversion was the work, primarily, of the Spirit within us. Sanctification, like redemption, is an ongoing process of change and must be worked out in the life of community. Like the mendicant alternative vow, that of poverty, this can be experienced in a life of service to others. As we serve the poor, we too are served by them. Opening our hearts to others in hospitality will bring about an internal change in us.

We could write several books exchanging different combinations of monastic virtues/vows with practices and exploring them within the theological narrative outlined in this book. Although I acknowledged the possibility of interchanging the monastic virtues/vows and practices, however, I didn't say the same about the theological narrative and it is on this point that I want to begin our conclusion.

Where one begins their theology is significant and sets the course of further discovery and thinking. I am increasingly convinced by Hugh of St Victor, who we have met before, and Karl Rahner, a 20th century Catholic theologian, amongst others as they begin in the only place we can: creation. We can only start where we know and move towards that which we do not. It is also the place where Scripture begins its articulation of the revelation of God Himself.

Hugh of St Victor offers a schema in his work, De Tribus Diebus, three days which an individual soul passes through on the journey to restoration: the day of the Father, the day of the Son and the day of the Holy Spirit. These three days stand as a narrative structure seen in the large story of history and experienced in the real lives of believers. It is this same three stage narrative that we have adopted and journeyed through together.

The first day begins with contemplating creation and acknowledging the power of God.

> ...when, therefore, the omnipotence of God is considered and arouses our heart to wonder, it is the day of the Father.[210]

The student 'who remembers where he was and recognizes where he is, may be led perhaps to see from his own case how through God's mercy man is brought from afar, and reintegrated after being scattered abroad.'[211] This then leads to the second day in which we are caused to reflect on the wisdom of God and on Truth itself. It is for this reason it is called the day of the Son for on

[210] Hugh of St Victor, *De Tribus Deibus*, 27.4
[211] Hugh of St Victor, *De Arca Noe*, 4,5

this day we are buried with Christ to the cares of the world and become alive only to God. As we fear the power of God we are humbled to see the truth of the wisdom of God.

Once we've experienced the power of God in creation and the wisdom of God in our redemption from the sin that has blinded us to Truth, we arrive at the third day: the day of the Spirit. On this third day we find ourselves reflecting on goodness and on morally applying what we have learnt from wisdom and being transformed into His likeness. This is the age to bear fruits of contemplation on wisdom and conversion from evil.

For Hugh of St Victor, the triad of power, wisdom and goodness should be at the very heart of our understanding of God as, sacred community. When we speak of Father, Son and Spirit we are talking also of Power, Wisdom and Goodness. I raise this so as to invite us to always seek to name an attribute of one person of the Godhead to the united whole, as Hugh himself clearly states.

> So power is of the Father, and is of the Son, and is of the Holy Ghost, and is properly and equally so; wisdom is of the Son, and is of the Father, and is of the Holy Ghost, and is properly and equally so; and love or goodness is of the Holy Ghost, and is of the Father, and is of the Son, and is properly and equally so. Because for God to have is the same as to be, and all that is in God can not be other than God, the Father is power, and the Son is power, and the Holy Ghost is power, and one power becomes one essence.[212]

It is useful to encounter the three persons in turn in order to appreciate the divinity of each and to see the fullness of God reflected in Them, but it is not good to remain distinguishing Them in this way forever. Like the journey we have been on it starts with

[212] Hugh of St Victor, *De Sacramentis*, 1.3.27

singularity, discovers multiplicity and concludes here in the balance of both.

*

Although this book seems directed primarily at those exploring the New Monastic movement, I hope, as I said at the beginning, it will also be beneficial to the whole of God's Church. Indeed, it is the proposition that the New Monastic movement might be a catalyst for renewal and reform within the Church that excites me most and has been my implicit proposal throughout the writing. This can only happen, however, if we acknowledge and understand the work God is calling us to as New Monastics and what treasures we offer to our brothers and sisters.

I suggest, like the renewal movement of the twelfth century, it focuses on a fresh engagement with the theology of the Trinity. We must refuse to allow this engagement to be rushed and shallow, but we must invest time and considered contemplation in the revealed truth of God as sacred community. As we appreciate afresh the triune nature of the Divine, we may find it shaping us into His likeness, not just individually but corporately. This is not to be a functional application but a sacramental indwelling as we experience the perichoretic life in our very being. It is this aim that I hope to have inspired in us all.

Again, it is in the work of Hugh of St Victor that I see a synthetic approach that I am discovering as I listen and relate to different communities that identify as New Monastic. In an increasing polarized culture, the renewal and reform programme lived out in the abbey of St Victor speaks to us of bringing together the gifts of both the 'secular' and the monastic life. As Dominique Poirel suggests, the Augustine canon regulars, of which Hugh was one, played the role of 'intermediary' between the secular 'masters' and the monastic life drawing on both.[213] It is in this role between

[213] Dominique Poirel, "Scholastic Reasons, Monastic Meditations and Victorine Conciliations: the Question of the unity and Plurality of God in the Twelfth Century",

the 'secular' parishes and the traditional religious life that New Monasticism seems to sit most naturally.

The Victorine school exemplified a form of hybrid between the clerical reforms being pursued by Pope Gregory VII and the monastic reforms epitomized by the Cistercians. This placed them in the between place between the two reform programmes.

> The canon regulars…were distinguished from their secular counterparts by their common life of shared property and their submission to the so-called 'Rule of St Augustine'. At the same time, in certain respects, they forged an identity in contrast to traditional monasticism. The canon regular "fell in between these two branches [clerical and monastic reform] and looked to both for inspiration."[214] [215]

The New Monastic movement finds itself consistently caught between the 'secular' church and the monastic tradition and feeling neither one thing nor the other. It is this sense of being between the cracks of these two bodies that makes our existence so hard to define and acknowledge. This tension, however, should not be avoided. Like the Victorines in the twelfth century so we, in the twenty-first century, are surely being called to embrace the intermediary, synthesizing role to see reform and renewal in both the 'secular' Church and the monastic tradition. This is a role we have not, I feel, fully adopted and it is one that I propose we articulate clearly to our brothers and sisters on either side of us.

To our 'secular' siblings we should actively and explicitly seek to publicize the treasures of faith, spirituality and discipleship that are held in the religious life and to encourage the teaching of the

---

Giles Emery O.P. and Matthew Levering (eds), *The Oxford Handbook of the Trinity* (Oxford: Oxford University Press, 2011) p.168

[214] Margot Fassler, *Gothic Song: Victorine Sequences and Augustinian Reform in Twelfth-Century Paris* (Cambridge: Cambridge University Press, 1993) p.187-240

[215] Coolman, *The Theology of Hugh of St Victor*, p.8

wider Church in the spiritual realities at work in this form of vocation. This could be expressed, as has been seen in the Community of St Anselm in Lambeth Palace, by giving opportunity for Christians to experience life in this form of community. I see, very much, the role of New Monastic communities being gateways into the traditional monastic houses and to encourage the growth in vocations to the religious life. We must acknowledge, however, that what we are being called to live is distinct from the traditional religious life. It has been, unhelpfully and patronizingly, described as 'Monasticism Lite' but we must continually acknowledge, to ourselves and others, that we are living 'a new form of monasticism' that is different from the other. We should embrace the task set out by Bonhoeffer to bring the radical discipleship and way of life from the cloisters into every ecclesial community and individual Christian life.

We have reflected on the need for the Church today to face the dilution of public vows within our life together. The lack of commitment within marital, baptismal and ordination vows has led, in part, to a distortion and weakness in our discipleship. The monastic vows to stability, conversion and obedience gives some language to the necessary conversations about this paucity. This does not mean, however, that I am arguing that all Christians should take on monastic vows but we should certainly take the treasures of this exemplar life to inform our own lives. Just as those who marry are to be a 'sign of unity and loyalty'[216] to all people, those who are baptized are to be a sign of new life to all people and those ordained to diaconal, presbyterial and episcopal orders are to be a sign of the servant, priestly and unity of all God's people, so should the devoted life be a sign to the whole Church of Christ.

The distinction between New Monasticism and traditional forms of religious life is an intentional commitment to the everyday, mixed life of contemplation and action. The canon regulars were urban dwellers, living in the midst of the hustle and

[216] The Archbishops' Council, *Common Worship: Pastoral Services*, p.105

bustle of ordinary life. Theirs was not a retreat but rather a public incarnation. One of the practical ways in which this is expressed is the inclusion of family life into the communities. Children are assumed to be present as well as married partners. In this way the discipleship encouraged in the religious life is not excluded to the cloisters but can, in part, without detracting from the unique cost and expression of traditional vocation, be experienced and lived out by all Christians.

Again, Hugh of St Victor could be an example of New Monasticism in the twelfth century.

> Of particular relevance to Hugh's theology is the way in which the idea of reform came increasingly to entail the attempt, not to return to an earlier, traditional form of religious life, but to establish new and better forms.[217]

The 'better form' expressed here is not to say that New Monasticism is an attempt to be superior to the earlier, traditional form but that we should hope that by encouraging new vocations to the religious life that that form of Christian life will grow and develop and evolve and experience a reformation and renewal itself.

Carolyn Bynum articulates three ideals of the canonical movement: a conviction that the mixed life of contemplation and action is superior to the purely contemplative life, a particular emphasis on preaching and teaching and a new focus on sacraments and history.[218] This final ideal would need further unpacking in the work of Hugh of St Victor but it would be enough for now to highlight Hugh's view of a 'sacrament' as a physical object that holds spiritual Truth and could be seen as a vehicle/icon of God's grace and directs the observer to understand and know God. In this

---

[217] Coolman, *The Theology of Hugh of St Victor*, p.8-9

[218] Carolyn Walker Bynum, "The Spirituality of Regular Canons in the Twelfth Century," in *Jesus as Mother: studies in the spirituality of the High Middle Ages* (Berkeley: University of California Press, 1982) 22-58

way the canonical movement might have engaged in the dialogue, what we might now call the fulcrum, between the sacred and the secular (in common terms).

To our 'professed' siblings, New Monasticism should be an encouragement to engage in partnership with the universal Church and to step out from the shadows of the cloisters and remind God's people of the power of a life devoted to Christ. The future of the Religious Orders depends upon new vocations and these must start with becoming visible and prophetic voices in a world in desperate need of authentic humility, love and grace. The renewal and reform programme in England during the 18th and 19th century saw the birth of the new forms of monasticism within the Church of England, the first since the dissolutions of the monasteries at the Reformation. The Oxford Movement was not merely about a ritualistic worship or vestments. At its heart it was a call to return to the basis of our faith. These communities looked to the universal truth of the Gospel and lived a form of life that would enable them to grow to full maturity and bring the Kingdom of God into the reality of those who desperately needed it.

This leads me to a final proposal for the role of New Monasticism in the renewal and reform of the religious life both in the secular Church and the professed communities.

> A set of values as well as a way of life, embodied in various institutions was at the heart of the movement of reform, which can be seen as an effort to monasticize first the clergy, by imposing on them a standard of life previously reserved for monks, and then the entire world.[219]

---

[219] Giles Constable, The Reformation of the Twelfth Century (Cambridge: Cambridge University Press, 1996) p. 3

I have always been interested in the way in which the monastic life could shape my own ministry as a clergy in the 'secular' parish. Many other clergy are feeling called to explore what I, unhelpful coined, 'Parish Monasticism'. This has led to many to ask the question; could an Anglican parish church create and adopt a Rule of Life? I, myself, have asked the same question and came to the conclusion: no.

The reason that I reached that conclusion was due to the impossibility of the discipline needed in the parish. If a Rule of Life is to be lived, it must be both communal and obeyed. The Church of England's ecclesiology has no means by which to enforce discipline on individual members of a church community (except its clergy). In establishing a parish/diocesan Rule of Life, therefore, one must either exclude many current members from membership to the common life desired and expressed, or eradicate any enforceable discipline and accountability to the Rule. What has occurred, therefore, in the examples currently being used is that it becomes an individual endeavor to develop an autonomous, personally shaped Rule not shared with others communally or shared but only under broad headings, or it's a communal life with no discernable discipline.

At the heart of the shared life under a Rule is the freely chosen commitment to that way of life and to the others under the Rule. The choice to commit must be done in the same manner by which God offered us a life of obedience. It is, as we have explored, the necessity of options that makes a choice free and full. Without the chance or capability to refuse there is no choice made. This does not mean, however, that part of a parish/diocese cannot commit to a shared Rule of Life, but there must be a clear articulation of authority and discipline to assist members to understand and experience stability, conversion of life and obedience, otherwise the religious life has little to no discernible impact on them. Those of the parish/diocese that do not choose to commit to a shared way of life can be treated as the lay members of monasteries who lived and worked alongside the devoted monks/nuns but were excluded from membership, due to their choice, from the specific community living under their Rule. This means that the 'parish'/'diocese' cannot become, in that way a religious community but rather should birth a religious community to live alongside the parish/diocese. In this way traditional religious communities could fulfill this role rather than birthing something totally new.

In questioning parochial/diocesan Rules of Life I am not rejecting the need for some form of shared principles and priorities; this is much needed and to be encouraged. Nor am I refuting the need to encourage a deeper commitment to the life of discipleship. I am merely questioning the simple and nominal adoption of a supposed 'Rule of Life' across a parish/diocese without any thought to the necessary authority required for a Rule of Life to impact its followers. New Monasticism could bless the Church by birthing new communities of clergy and laity within parochial and diocesan structures, as prophetic signs of devotion. This will encourage some clergy to be 'monasticised' but how might we, as New Monastics, further encourage the monasticizing of clergy?

If there is, as I have suggested, a diluting of the vows made within the Church (baptismal, marital and ordination) then, as I have subtly outlined in each section of this book, the uncompromising religious life can inspire a recommitment to them. Religious communities should be a prophetic sign to the rest of the Church, pointing to the radical submission to the will of God for the flourishing of all creation. The Church needs, before all else, to recapture that whole life commitment to the vows we make to one another in the sight of God. Just as the vows of marriage are to be a sign to others to the life of chastity and stability, just as the vows of baptism are to be a sign to others to the life of conversion, and just as the vows of ordination are to be a sign to others to the life of obedience, so the vows made by the religious life are to be a sign to others of a shared life of prayer, study and service to others.

Finally, clergy have already, publicly committed to obedience in their ordination vows. There is a way in which New Monasticism could impact the Church by encouraging bishops to take on the authority invested in them to become abbot/abbess like figures within their diocese. To gather their ordained brothers and sisters around them and committing to one another under a Rule of Life. This would be a bold and radical venture. As I have said, it would require all clergy to choose to commit to it or some will be, necessarily excluded from the community, but it might shift the life of that diocese. In order to ensure the clergy are living out that life, publicly, they might gather round them lay members in their locality/parish and birth small communities within the diocesan community. This strategy, however, would require the bishop to think through, fully, the ramifications of obedience within the diocese and through the parishes.

It is disheartening to experience, again and again, gatherings of these new forms of ecclesial communities, as confusion and conflict leads to polarizing language on either/or. Despite the many utterances of 'both/and' this rarely gets worked out or codified. To conclude, therefore, I return to the beauty of the Trinitarian life of God. In the three persons there is no conflict or inequality. It is in the three authorities and the mutual, perichoretic love between them that division is avoided in the mysterious existence of the revealed Triune God. It is the shaping of ideas and communities around three points, rather than two, which brings a creative tension and expressed depth to our life and reality.

New Monasticism, I suggest, does not merely 'fall between two branches' but adds a third dimension to the life of God's Body which enhances and seeks the flourishing of the other two parts. It also, in itself, hold many triads of principles, practices and authorities to ensure it remains fruitful. In our journey from Ash to Water to Oil we have seen that each of these made up of three aspects, which could be expressed as that Deuteronomic prayer, 'love the Lord your God with all your heart, and with all your soul and with all your might.'

To love God with all your heart, in Hebraic terms is to utilize the mind. It is in this way that the intellect and study becomes a form of loving God. Study is to be seen as an act of worship. In our journey, it is in engaging in the narrative of our faith, the study of Creation, Redemption and Sanctification and in our desire to know and live out that one story that becomes one way of loving God. This is about taking orthodoxy seriously.

To love God with all your soul is about engaging and directing our desires and emotions towards God in an appropriate and right way. What we feel, particularly on a sub-conscious level directs our actions and response to the world. Being mindful and conscious of these powerful impulses and placing under the authority of God to shape for His purposes is a profound and difficult act of submission. In our journey, it is in engaging with the commitment to Stability, Conversion and Obedience and allowing these to reform our very beings that becomes another way of loving God. This is about taking orthopathy seriously.

Finally, to love God with all your might is to use our bodies and actions in service to, with and for God. Our life is nothing if not performed belief. What we say and think is hollow if it is not seen meted out in our active life. In our journey, it is in engaging in the practices of Prayer, Study and Service and a balanced commitment to invest time and effort into all three that becomes the final way of loving God. This is about taking orthopraxis seriously.

To commit our whole lives to God is to ensure each aspect is given to Him; our thoughts, our feelings and our actions. Indeed, it is even in how these interact one with another that drives us deeper into relationship with Him and, at the same time, is the way in which He will work His transforming love into our lives. This triune experience of love is, in the mystery of our Trinitarian faith, synonymous with the proclamation and belief in the unity of the Divine and the truth that 'The Lord is our God.'

The final word then should be a simple answer posed by this book: why does the Church need a new form of monasticism? Whenever God's people lose their way and find themselves unduly yoked to a crumbling culture, God sends prophets to remind the people of the past, to speak eternal truths into the present, to live, uncompromisingly as though the future Kingdom were present today and to be a signpost to that coming Kingdom. Since Antony and the Desert Fathers and Mothers, that life has been called 'monasticism'… The Church needs this because it always needs it.

Printed in Great Britain
by Amazon